Zintgraff's Explorations
in Bamenda, Adamawa and the Benue Lands
1889—1892

Dr Eugen Zintgraff and his dog

Zintgraff's Explorations in Bamenda, Adamawa and the Benue Lands

1889—1892

E. M. Chilver

Langaa Research & Publishing CIG
Mankon, Bamenda

Publisher:
Langaa RPCIG
Langaa Research & Publishing Common Initiative Group
P.O. Box 902 Mankon
Bamenda
North West Region
Cameroon
Langaagrp@gmail.com
www.langaa-rpcig.net

Distributed outside N. America by African Books Collective
orders@africanbookscollective.com
www.africanbookscollective.com

Distributed in N. America by Michigan State University Press
msupress@msu.edu
www.msupress.msu.edu

ISBN: 9956-616-71-0

© E. M. Chilver 2010
First published, Buea, 1966, Reprinted by friends of the Buea archives, Oxford, 1996

DISCLAIMER

All views expressed in this publication are those of the author and do not necessarily reflect the views of Langaa RPCIG.

Contents

Preface vii
Introductory Notes xi

NORD-KAMERUN (Berlin 1895), by Eugen Zintgraff 1
    TO BABESSONG 1
    BALI 4
    THE FON GAREGA 6
    THE STATION 10
    THE FON AND HIS PEOPLE 12
    BALI LIFE 16
    DEPARTURE 19
    MANKON AND BAFUT 21
    THE MARCH CONTINUES 27
    TAKUM AND THE BENUE LANDS 29
    THE RETURN THROUGH ADAMAWA 31
    TAKUM, BUM, BIKOM 35
    BAMUNGU (BABUNGO) 38
    TO BALI VIA BAMBUI AND BAFRENG 40
    RETURN TO THE COAST 41
    REPORT TO GERMANY 42
    A NEW EXPEDITION 46

RETURN TO BALI 47
BAFUT AND MANKON 49
THE BATTLE OF MANKON 52
DISASTER 54
RE-ORGANIZATION 58
A TREATY WITH GAREGA 59
THE BALI-TRUPPE 62
PROGRESS 63
ZIMMERER'S OPPOSITION 64

Selected Bibliography 67

Preface

In 1961 Mrs Chilver prepared the following notes for limited circulation. With the inception of our new historical series, we have now found it possible to print them so that they may reach the wider audience they deserve.

Some clarificatory remarks upon the place-names and routes to be met with may be helpful. Zintgraff and his commercial companions travelled by water from Douala *(Duald)*, the seat of the Kamerun government, through the creeks and up the Mungo river to Mundame, a Balong village in the present Kumba Division. At Mundame there was a large depot. From there an overland carrier-route went through Mukonje to Mambanda, branching at Kumba to Barombi-Station, the first site of the government headquarters there. From Mambanda the route went north, through Ikiliwindi, and roughly followed the line of the present road as far as Nguti *(N'Guti's)*. Then it passed through Banyang country via the villages of Defang, Fotabe, Tinto, Tali and Sabe, climbing the escarpment to Ashong *(Babessong)* in Moghamo and then to Bali *(Baliburg)*. Zintgraff habitually used the chiefs' names as village-names on this part of the route and sometimes it is difficult to decide which are which. Thus *Difang (p.24)* the hostile Banyang chief was the chief of the modern village of Defang which was named after him. *Fo Tabe* (p.25) is used as the name both of the chief and of the village usually spelled Fotabe. Zintgraff built a station at the next village which he called *Miyimbi* (p.29) after its chief. This is the present village of Tali. Zintgraff took Chief Miyimbi's daughter to the grasslands where she died on the heights near Bambui (p.21).

The names of the Grassland section of the route are dealt with in the text but they may be summarized here for reference. *Baliburg* was the station established by Zintgraff outside Bali town. Bangwa or *Bangoa* was a village nearby, which defected at the Battle of Mankon; it should not be confused with the Bangwa of Mamfe Division. Mankon is referred to throughout Zintgraff's text as *Bandeng*, a form of *Bande*, the Bali-derived name by which it was popularly known until recent years. The form *Mankon* is used in the headings of the present volume, but the form *Bande* is used when citing Zintgraff.

Bafuen is Bafreng (Nkwen). This is also spelt *Bafren* in Zintgraff's official reports. *Munda* or *Bamunda* is Menda Nkwe, the village which owned the present site of Bamenda station. Hutter gives its population then as 3,000. *Bamungu* is Babungo. Bambui and Bafut are spelt as today. *Bafum* was the general name by which the Benue people knew most of the present Wum Division. In the text it refers to Bum.

On Zintgraff's outward route the name *Babeumka* is not clearly identifiable. In geographical position, we should expect Wum, as Mrs Chilver suggests (p. 15). It might at this period possibly be Esu (otherwise known as Bafumkatse). The name *Menka'* or *Nka'* (from which comes the modern spelling *Munkap* and the like) may be an old general name for the western Esu chiefdom, now restricted to specific villages, including two now in Esu territory. Thus Bafum-nka or Babe-nka are possibilities. In the Benue area, *Okari* is Wukari; *Ashaku* is Utsuku. When Zintgraff speaks of crossing the Katsina Ala River on his way back from Takum he is mistaken, as he actually crossed the Gamana: the more northerly of the two rivers shown in the map on p.xiii.

The map of Zintgraff's routes has been redrawn upon a modern base, with place-names in present-day spelling. The map of the battle of Mankon is based upon one published in his book. The plates are reproduced from those of Zintgraff.

Once more, for technical reasons the German *umlaut* cannot be used and to enable the accurate citation of proper names from this booklet we give here the names found in the main text which should bear umlauts (the umlauted vowels are shown by the addition of an *e*):

Hutter—Huetter;
Bockner—Boeckner;
Thormahlen—Thormaehlen;
Steinacker—Steinaecker;
Goger—Goeger

The headings to be found in the text of Zintgraff have been added for the convenience of the reader.

The arrangements for the reproduction of the plates, which are an excellent feature of this publication, were made by S. G. Ardener, also of U. K. Technical Assistance. The work was undertaken by City Engraving Ltd of Hull, England. Special acknowledgement must be made to the Government Printer, Mr T. Betteridge, and his staff at all levels for their advice and unflagging interest, and for the technical skill they have put into this production. For this reason I hope that they will forgive this breach of their traditional anonymity.

Edwin W. Ardener

Introductory Notes

The following pages contain brief extracts and summaries of those parts of Eugen Zintgraff's book *Nord-Kamerun* (1895), which we thought would be of most interest concerning Bamenda and Wum Division. The book, the first by a European about the Grassfields, has not been translated and is hard to get second-hand.

In using these notes the following points should be borne in mind: Zintgraff's knowledge of Bali *(Mungaka)* and Hausa was very slight, and his discussions of character, motives and political institutions are consequently superficial and open to criticisms. He had no means of checking what he was told, or thought he was told. He had no previous knowledge of any similar culture and no training in ethnographical method. He was, however, a good observer, and his descriptions of tools, dress, weapons and the like, can be regarded as fairly reliable. Finally, it must be remembered that Zintgraff wrote the book to justify his own actions and to support that small but influential section of public opinion in Germany which favoured rapid imperial expansion. A full account of the actions and motives of Zintgraff's opponents in the Kamerun Government and in the Colonial Bureau of the German Foreign Office has not been written: we only have one side of the story. But there are some suggestive points made in Rudin's *Germans in the Cameroons* and I shall refer to others below.

Zintgraff's career

Eugen Zintgraff was born in Dusseldorf, Germany, in 1858. In 1884 he accompanied the explorer Chavanne to the Lower Congo. In 1886 he entered the service of the German Government, but was unable to persuade it to support his plan to explore Kamerun from the direction of the Ubangi river to the coast. In 1886/7 he made some probing expeditions round the Kamerun (Wouri) estuary. In January 1888 he established the Barombi (Kumba) Station with Zeuner, from there pushing forward into the eastern Banyang area of the present Mamfe Division. He reached Bali in January 1889. The summary takes the story to 1892. In 1893 he went to South Africa as a journalist. He returned to Kamerun in 1896, with Dr Max Esser, as manager of the Victoria plantation (W.A.P.V.), and accompanied him to Bali in that year to make an agreement with Fon Garega I, for the supply of plantation labour. Zintgraff died in December, 1897, off Teneriffe in the Canary Islands on the way home on sick-leave.

Franz Hutter

Something should also be said about the Bavarian officer, Hutter, who was temporarily left in charge of the Baliburg station until the beginning of 1893. He was born in 1865, and joined Zintgraff in 1891 as a young artillery Lieutenant. In 1904-5 he made further explorations in Kamerun, as a company employee. He published a book in 1902 about his experiences with Zintgraff which add some further detail to Zintgraff's account for 1891-2, and some useful material on the relations between Bali and nearby chiefdoms. He, like Zintgraff, looked back with nostalgia to his time in Baliburg.

Links with the Coast

The link with the Coast established by Zintgraff did not disappear with the departure of Hutter. As we have seen, a W.A.P.V. expedition reached Bali in 1896 and before and after that the German trader and W.A.P.V. labour-recruiter Conrau was active on the Bali road, until 1899, when he was murdered with his Bali companion in confused circumstances while on a recruiting tour, by the Fontem people. His death brought up punitive patrols, now supported in the rear by the Station at Johann-Albrechtshohe (Kumba). Meanwhile people from the Grassfields had found their way to the Coast, some in Conrau's employment, some in W.A.P.V. and other plantation service, or in the service of the government. Following the labour-supply treaty between W.A.P.V. and Fon Garega in 1896, in June 1897 over 100 Bali had arrived in Victoria to work in Zintgraff's concern. Other contingents followed. In 1900, the general agent of the North-West Kamerun Company, Captain Ramsay, arrived in Bali to negotiate a trading concession. In May, 1901, a large Bali embassy reached Buea to report formally the accession of Fon Fonyonga II, and were received by Governor von Puttkamer. By the end of that year a military expedition under Lt. Col. Pavel had defeated the Bangwa, then Mankon and Bafut, with the help of a column brought up from the Cross River by Captain Glauning, and broke through unexplored country beyond Babungo to Banyo early in 1902. By 1902 the foundations of the German military station at Bamenda had been laid, and a new chapter had begun.

Some criticisms of Zintgraff's policy

Zintgraff was criticised on several counts. One set of critics had political doubts. Rittmeister von Stetten, first head of the Schutztruppe, who visited Bali for 15 days at the end of 1892, thought that the political situation in Bali was tricky because of the enmity of surrounding peoples. Conrau, who visited Bali at the end of 1893 noted the rivalry between Tita N'ji and Garega's choice, Tita M'bo, which, he thought, might weaken Bali after Fon Garega's death. A weakened Bali, with watchful enemies, would not be a useful prop for German administration. Tita N'ji (Tita N'yi) in fact predeceased Fon Garega; M'bo became Fonyonga II (in his princely days he was also referred to as Tita Gwenjang). Von Stetten, moreover, was doubtful whether the Bali would make good labourers for the plantations, though they might make good soldiers and station employees.

The economic argument against Zintgraff's policy is fairly put by his friend Max Esser. The four stations on the Bali road cost about 80,000 marks a year to run, while the value of the produce brought in for sale to Mundame was at most 25,000 marks a year. Indeed, after the Baliburg and other stations had been given up, the produce trade had not diminished but had been slightly increased. So, argued Esser, the stations, which were supposed to protect and encourage trade, were unnecessary at the time, and it would be better to concentrate Government investment on the Coast, as the Portuguese had done in their colonies. At this time, it must be remembered, Kamerun was costing the German taxpayer money and had to be subsidised.

A third critic was Zintgraff's employee, the road builder Bockner, previously employed at the Botanic Gardens. Bockner, in newspaper articles, roundly accused Zintgraff of carelessness and maladministration, and some of his associates, particularly Freiherr von Gemmingen, of brutality. The deserted state of the route, he said, was due to high-handed treatment of the villagers by Zintgraff's inexperienced subordinates, and depre-dations by deserting carriers, who were making a good thing out of selling arms. The carriers' desertions were due to excessive punishments and bad pay. The Vai-boys from Liberia were not properly controlled: some were favourites, others deserted in desperation. The deserted state of the route forced Bali messengers to raid villages for food, and Bockner had to intervene between them and the raided villagers. The carelessness over weapons had led to their wide dissemination and to increased insecurity. Bockner did not publish his report until early in 1893, but if reports such as this had reached the Coast in 1892, the Governor Zimmerer's 'coldness' towards Zintgraff is understandable. Von Stetten's report, previously referred to, also makes discreet refe-rences to the bad relations along the route.

Finally, there were commercial critics who thought that plunging into the interior was economically rash and politically unwise. The head of the main rival to Jantzen and Thormahlen: Woermann & Co. believed in gradual penetration and thought that unarmed missionaries were better heralds of European culture than armed expeditions. Others thought that African traders working on credit were more efficient and less expensive than European agents, who were hard to recruit and sickened easily.

One of the consequences of Zintgraff activity was the recruitment of inland labour for the plantations—though this would have happened in any event. While this built up the Cameroons economy, it led to many deaths among the labourers unused to the climate, diet and conditions of the Coast and often exhausted by their journey. Epi-demics flourished in crowded and insanitary labour lines, among ill-nourished men. Some labourers went quite willingly; others were recruited by forceful methods, or collected after punitive expeditions. Conditions improved in time; missionaries, their political allies in Germany, and the Socialists exposed scandals and agitated for the careful treatment of labour, and some plantations had a good reputation with their employees.

It is perhaps worth considering whether development in the Cameroons would have been faster or slower without the plantations, and what would have happened if the British Northern Nigerian policy of slow peasant development had been adopted by the Germans. Would the rather rigid division of labour between men and women have held back the early development of cash crops in Bamenda? And was the problem of transportation to the Coast insuperable?

Some suggestions for research

There are still old people alive who remember Zintgraff, but he is sometimes confused with later German visitors. Some description of him may be useful therefore. He was not a big man, was very light-complexioned, and wore spectacles. On his journeys he wore a broad-brimmed hat, turned up in front, light woollen clothing, and high boots reaching above the knee, till these wore out. During his stay in the Grassfields he grew a small beard, and wore moustaches. He went everywhere with his dog, black with a white muzzle and paws.

Hutter was a bigger and stronger fellow, with a darker beard, who wore a bush hat, uniform bush-jacket and high boots. He also had spectacles. He was about 26 when he arrived in Bali. He is sometimes confused with Hauptmann Glauning (1901-8) who had no beard, no spectacles, piercing blue eyes, and wore the red shoulder tabs of the Schutztruppe (the Protectorate Force). One of his successors, Adametz, is well remembered for his great size, enormous feet, and cheerful and decisive manner. But these were not the only 'Kammendas' or 'Hauptmanns' of note: people may re-member Strumpell, interested in languages and customs, Menzel, von Raven and von Sommerfeld, all much later than Hutter.

In collecting historical material about the first German penetration—dealt with in this note—whether Zintgraff or someone later is meant can be fixed rather more closely by asking what he looked like, whether he was the chief man at Baliburg, whether Fon Garega I was still alive and whether the events occurred *before* the Germans founded Bamenda Station. The only other explorers known to have been near Bamenda or Wum before 1901, besides those we have mentioned in these notes and the extracts, were the Englishmen Hewby and Moseley: of these two, Moseley reached Bum, while Hewby remained on the borders. Both came down from Kentu with Hausa companions. There was possibly an ivory poacher also. Zintgraff's predecessor Flegel reached Berabe, Banyo and Takum: he went by the name of Abder-Rahman and wore Hausa dress, but was dead before Zintgraff appeared.

While the history of German exploration is interesting in itself, and important as setting in train the events which brought Cameroonians together into a larger whole, it is also important for the light it throws on local history. Who, for example, was Chief of Bambui when Zintgraff's expedition met such terrible weather coming up from Babungo, and where did they cross the mountains? What and where was Babeumka? Who was the chief of Bangola who came to Babungo? Is Ndeng the same as Achan or some other place? Who was the trusty retainer who negotiated on behalf of Fon Mboombi (Gualem) of Bafut with Zintgraff? Who was the Mankon standard-bearer killed by Zintgraff? Who was the 'clever old sub-chief who led the centre of the Bali force in the attack on Mankon? What was the usual route for traders going to Takum? These questions and others should not be too difficult to answer: others of local interest can be posed.

What is perhaps most striking about Zintgraff's account is the fact that the people of the Western Grassfields were not so isolated from one another or their neighbours as might be thought. At Babungo Zintgraff could discuss how best to reach Banyo, at Takum how to reach 'Bafum.' A network of trade-friendships covered the country and big men exchanged gifts over long distances. These links must be set beside the insecurity due to raids and slave-catching, and are well worth investigation.

E. M. Chilver

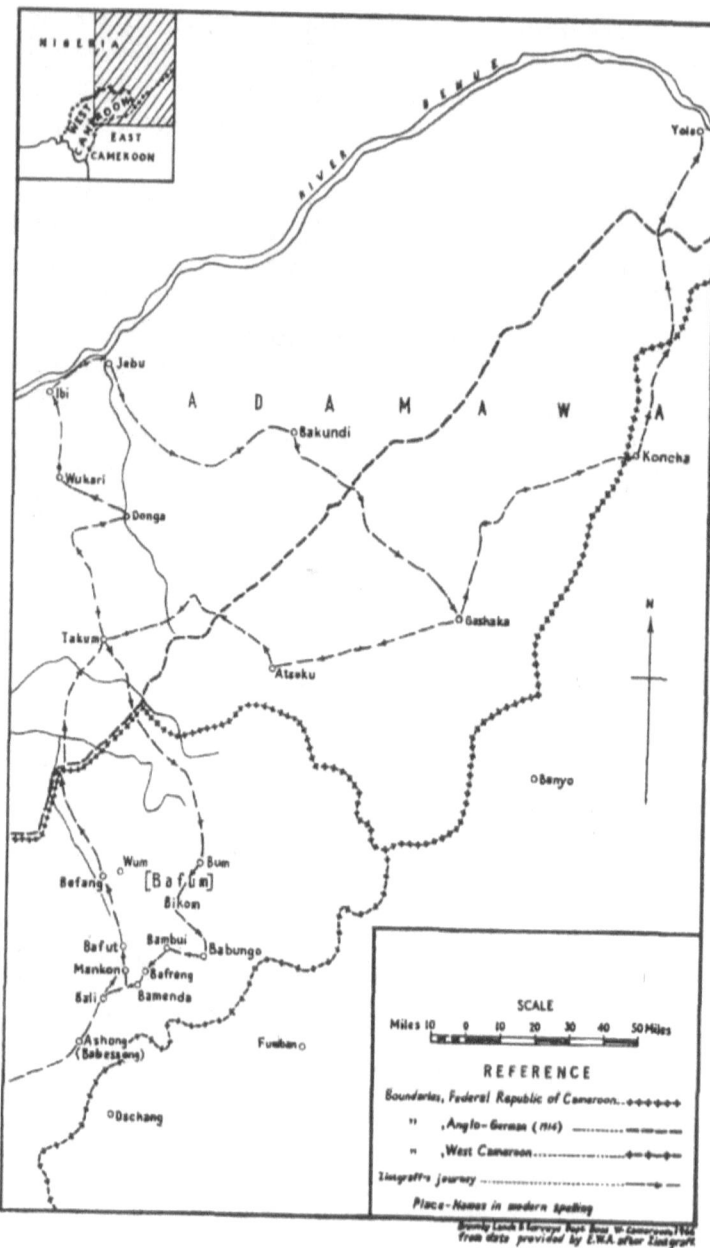

Zintgraff's Explorations in Bamenda, Adamawa and the Benue Lands

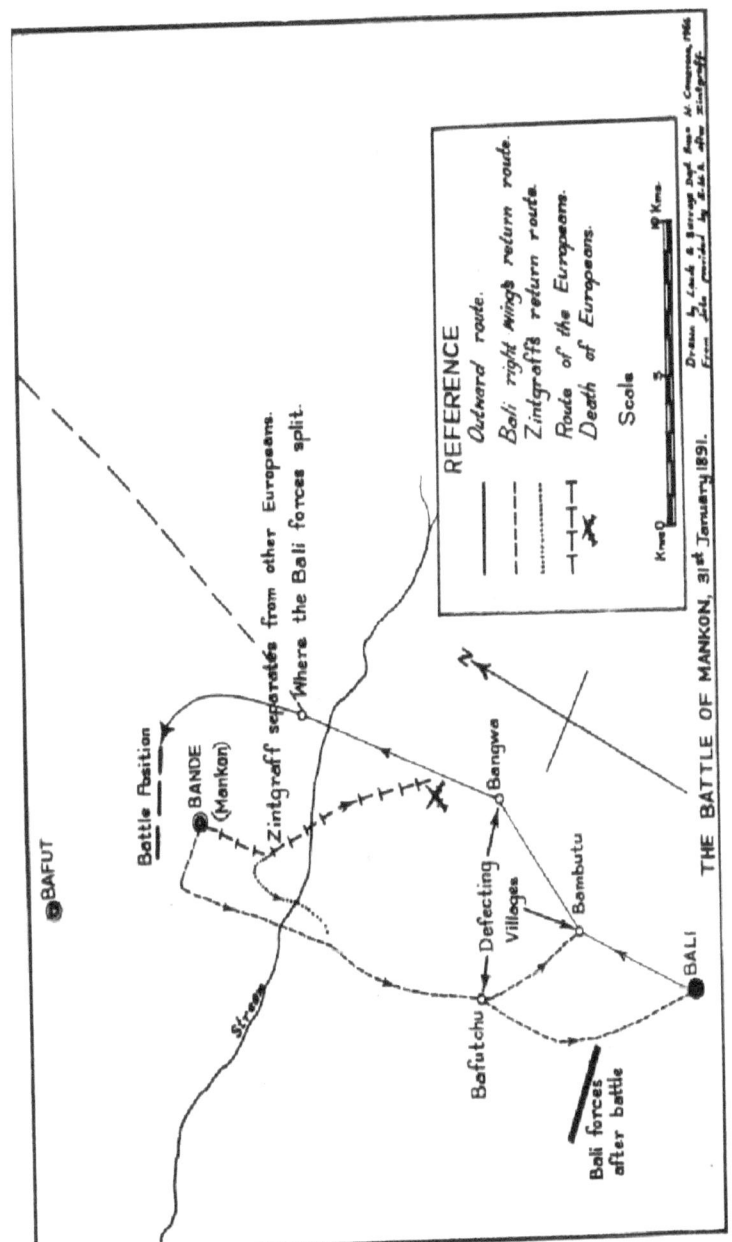

NORD-KAMERUN (Berlin 1895) by Eugen Zintgraff

N.B.—In this precis of Nord-Kamerun the passages in italics are summaries, and those between inverted commas are free and condensed translations of the text. Omissions within paragraphs have been indicated by punctuation marks. Omissions at the end of paragraphs or between paragraphs have not been indicated. Some place-names have been modernized.

TO BABESSONG

Zintgraff's second attempt to penetrate to Adamawa from the coast in July-August 1888 took him as far as Banyang country. He had an interpreter, one Muyenga, a slave of Manga Bell's, who came from Bayong country in the 'far hinterland.' In January 1889 he climbed to the plateau having passed through Tali and Sabi. The first Grassfield people he met with, Zintgraff calls Babe, under Fon M'bere. This was not far from Babessong, under Nu Taku. Two envoys from Fo Bessong met him with palmwine andkolas and took him to their chief. Zintgraff remarks that there were hardly any guns to be seen, a contrast with the people living near the Cross River.

'Babessong was one of the dirtiest places I have seen in Africa not only with regard to the exteriors of the old smoke-blackened houses with their moss-covered roofs, but as regards the streets which were wallows for numerous pigs... Finally the chief appeared from a compound set away to one side. Round his hips he wore a long skirt-like loin-cloth and on his head a red executioner's cap with ear-flaps, decorated with a long cock's feather. He was a tall figure with an elastic gait, and the few grey hairs in his thin beard proclaimed him past his manly prime.'

Fo Bessong after looking at Zintgraff in astonishment greeted him warmly, asked him his plans and then led him to a better house near the market place. A fog descended—meanwhile people streamed in to the market place to dance what Zintgraff calls a 'sword-dance', clashing their cutlasses and stamping to the sound of the big war-drums. Muyenga advised Zintgraff that the situation was tricky. In the afternoon a sub-chief whose village had been passed en route came in and told Fo Bessong excitedly that Zintgraff should go no further. Zintgraff decided to win Fo Bessong over with gifts and gave him an artillery-man's coat, three pieces of cloth and some bundles of tobacco. Fo Bessong was a great snuff-taker. Zintgraff describes him as carrying a polished drinking-horn from which he poured palmwine into the horns of his close associates as a favour.

Next morning Fo Bessong gave Zintgraff a pig, and provided a little food and at least a hundred litres of palmwine. A big war-dance was put on. Zintgraff was impressed by the singing and the dexterity and vehemence of the dance, and notes the difference in physique between the 'flabby fellows in the warm forest' and the 'lively, strong, highland lads'. The chief took part in the dance, wearing the blue coat Zintgraff had given him, later changing to a fine robe somewhat like a Hausa gown but different in detail.

'We saw three of the before-mentioned Bali; they vanished in the afternoon apparently to give their chief, living a day's march away, a report about us.'

Zintgraff remarks that everything was done here to the accompaniment of feasting and singing. Everyone carried a bush-cow horn or calabash vessel in a fibre bag. Whenever the chief sat, a huge palmwine jug was set beside him. Frequently before drinking, a few drops were poured on the earth as an offering. The chief was treated with outward respect, people speaking softly in his presence. He sat on a carved stool while his brother and some of his councillors squatted on the ground. In the afternoon many of the sur-rounding chiefs came in, some to bring gifts, others to persuade Fo Bessong to kill Zintgraff, capture his carriers and sell them as slaves.

Fo Bessong discussed his predicament frankly with Zintgraff, who gave him an accordion which pleased him greatly, Zintgraff heard later that Fo Bessong had built a bamboo hut for it and would only play it if a gift was first made. On the third day of Zintgraff's stay two hundred men from a neighbouring hostile village came in armed: Fo Bessong gave them palmwine and nothing happened.

'The Bali chief... through the messengers we had fleetingly seen, sent us three elephants' feet and yams with an invitation to visit him. Following this we had a discussion about our passage in the evening. Fo Bessong declared he was ready to agree as he had had a fine gift and finally put my hand in those of his retainers and his frog-faced minister (his brother) as a sign that these would guide me. But he must await another message from Bali as the Bali chief could not yet see me on account of a death in his family.

In order to ensure that he was not being tricked Zintgraff, on Muyenga's advice, entered into a blood-pact with Fo Bessong. A paste of chewed kola and kubeb-pepper was placed on cuts made on their arms, and each had to lick it off. Blood from the cuts was mixed with palmwine and mutually drunk and a mutual oath of protection taken. Breaking the oath would mean that the oath breaker's belly would swell in 9 days and he would die horribly.

E. M. Chilver

BALI

On the next day, 16th January, 1889, after Fo Bessong had been given a ship's bell and some rockets as a parting gift, Zintgraff started with Fo Bessong's brother and retainers as guides. As he left Fo Bessong spat on Zintgraff's face and hands as a blessing. They walked along a well-marked path along hill-ridges from which settlements in the valleys could be seen. After two hours they rested in a shady valley, at a point half-way to Bali.

"Then we went a little way uphill and met the first messengers of the chief of Bali. These were about twenty warriors armed with spears and dane-guns led by three elders clad in shirt-like cloaks. The warriors were bare to the waist and wore an apron-like loin-cloth. Their spokesman, as envoy of the chief, carried a bundle of spears; the spearheads were covered in sheaths of black goatskin, decorated with red leather bands, as a symbol of peace.'

The Bali and Babessong parties sat down. The Bali party had brought Zintgraff a fine stool to sit on and a fly-whisk. Zintgraff noted the quiet self-possession of the Bali.

The Bali spokesman addressed Fo Bessong's brother as follows: 'The chief sent us to greet the white man of whose coming we had heard. From now on he is under our protection and he can trust us to lead him to Bali. He may like some food and drink to strengthen him.' Thus saying he drew out of his bag a calabash, decorated with burnt-on designs, full of palmwine, and some packets of essuga. Zintgraff remarks that for the first time he met Africans who looked at him straight in the eye. The spokesman now led the column, with three young lads. The party were concerned to obey the chiefs order to bring Zintgraff to Bali in safety and were always at hand to help him over stones and log-bridges.

'From a height about an hour distant from Bali we saw in a large, cultivated valley, the first farms of Bali. The few dark rocks in the foreground, and behind a silver-gleaming waterfall, together with the extensive fields, green banana groves and cottages, combined to present a peaceful picture, strange to me, yet homely.'

Another party with refreshments met Zintgraff and he noticed the prevalence of guinea-corn cultivation.

'A relatively deep stream, which we had seen from afar as a waterfall, ran through the valley; this we crossed on a bridge of tied logs in the middle of a fertile depression. Climbing the opposite slope, we met a welcoming and helpful crowd, with palmwine, showing a hospitality we had not encountered else where... The plan of the compounds was excellent; carefully woven mat walls surrounded the dozen or more cottages comprising them. A regular gate with a gable-roof led through these walls. Numerous men, women and children stood at the compound entrances or at the mouth of the lanes leading to the main road and greeted us cheerfully. After a 10 minute walk along this shady 1£ metre-broad road, and passing some small market-places where cloth, beads, pipes, mats etc. were sold, we turned a corner and came suddenly upon the main market-square where a most unexpected sight greeted us.

Before us, gently rising, lay a large open square, lined on two sides with huts, into which numerous lanes led from different directions. In front of us was the extensive compound of the chief, hidden by finely woven mat walls and overhung by shady trees. Before it, not far from a gate to the right, there arose, in the square itself, a large assembly house open on two sides. On the upper side of the square squatted about 2,000 warriors, their dane-guns and spears upright between their knees, in perfect silence. In the middle of the square was a turret-shaped pile of stones from the middle of which a pole with three branches at the top emerged.' Zintgraff was given a stool by his companions and sat down. After about half an hour some servants emerged to lay a big cowskin in front of him, and place a stool on it. Zintgraff notes that the 'rock throne' was on the left of the palace gate.

THE FON GAREGA

'Finally the chief appeared, crossing the high threshold of the gate with slow, measured tread. A big, well-fleshed figure, wearing a dark-red burnous whose ample folds increased his massiveness, he stood upright before his stone seat and looked at me keenly. Then he sat down while the assembled warriors clapped three times. After he had spoken a few words to his retainers he arose with an elastic but dignified step and came towards me. I arose and looked at him full in the face, which, I remarked, was not very negroid in feature. He looked at me for a moment and then suddenly seized my right wrist and raised my arm, and told his fifty or so elders that the white man's skin did not burn, as he had been told, and that he could not possibly have come up out of the water. Then he looked closely at my hand and fingers and seemed satisfied and pleased with his inspection. Then he sat beside me... while a servant came with heated palm-wine he, dividing a kola nut, gave me one half and ate the other. Then he had my cup filled with wine and after pouring a little on the earth, drank some and passed the cup to me. I copied his action. My elderly guides and the Babessong people then received their share. A festive round began while Fon Garega attentively listened to the tale of our journey.. .and expressed his astonishment at our arrival.'

Rain drove them indoors while Zintgraff's followers were brought into the assembly-house and given wine, food and firewood. Zintgraff himself was housed in a roomy clean house near Fon Garega's own, with a private drinking booth for the Fon. Here he was visited by the Forts two eldest sons, Titas N'yi and M'bo who watched the erection of his camp bed and field-kitchen with curiosity. Zintgraff remarks on the difference between the Fon of Sali and 'Bell, Akwa and Co.' and says that the behaviour of his carriers reflected their feeling that they were in the presence of a real chief.

Next day and on the following days Zintgraff explained that he wanted to go north to 'where people rode horses.' Garega was convinced that Zintgraff's carriers were slaves, and that he evidently wished to buy slaves and horses, which Garega offered to arrange if he stayed. Garega used to come and see Zintgraff privately in the evenings.

Fon Garega I

'On these occasions he wore the customary loincloth and was otherwise bare, except for a necklace of native work made from European brass. I had the opportunity to notice, with astonishment, that in spite of his sixty odd years, his figure was erect, powerful, and well-knit.

He said... that I would have to visit six chiefs en route and that it would be good if he 'bought the way' for me. I was struck by his remark that his father came from the very regions I was wanting to visit.'

Next day Zintgraff presented him with over three hundred metres of cloth, mirrors, etc. But Garega made no sign as regards guides or travel preparations. Zintgraff thought that Garega wanted to impress his neighbours by keeping him and his party with him, and also thought it likely that he feared that the 'Hausa' who had attacked his 'father' would be shown the way. Meanwhile the morale of the carriers had so declined that it would have been difficult in any event to press on. By degrees the idea of establishing a station at Bali began to impress itself on Zintgraff, who was impressed by the bearing of the Bali, the healthiness and fertility of the country and the nearness to sources of ivory. He began to see the Ball as allies.

'Naturally this point of view was thoroughly approved by Garega and he assured me that he would keep his word about my eventual departure. On the next day a big dance was held, so that the people could be informed on this occasion of the settlement of the white man. Then the Bali would build me the station and I would not have to lift a hand.

Garega took an oath on this agreement in customary fashion, and repeated it with my headman: after the killing of the goat, they rubbed each other with camwood.'

The news spread rapidly. People streamed in to the dance, for which hundreds of calabashes of wine were brought in by slaves. The general summons was given by ivory horns which were used to call the Bali to dance and to war. Garega sat on a stone, Zintgraff near him. The two horn-blowers were on the left. Next to them was the Bali flag of white native cotton, flown on a long lance, and the German red, white and black standard given by Zintgraff. These were with a guard of honour and nobody might approach the ground on which they stood. On the left of Garega stood his armed servants leaving a space free at the gate to the palace and round the flags. Next to them was the group under the redoubtable Tita N'yi, Garega's eldest son. On Garega's right was the group under his second son M'bo. In front of him a space was left free for the war-dance.

'To the sound of ivory horns and drumming the chief arose, on this occasion bare to the waist, a cutlass on his left flank and holding ia his right hand a dane-gun decorated with brass nails and amulets, surrounded by trusted retainers. Towards him came first his own warriors, led by the eldest officer, while his retainers leapt forward and placed themselves in front of him. Guns and spears were swung and presented. The advancing party proclaimed their courage, pounding their chests. In answer, Garega's bodyguard shook their feather-crowned heads violently. There was a threefold rush back and forth and the third time they took the chief between them and marched with him with long war-like strides till a halt was made in the middle of the market-place.

The hitherto confused crowd now divided itself into two long rows, with left knee bent, the right leg stretched out, guns raised and ready to spring. Some detached themselves, pretending to fight an imaginary enemy. Here and there shots rang out; cutlasses were drawn and imaginary enemies beheaded... Now they came forward to greet the chief.'

Zintgraff notes the particular energy of Tita N'yi, Garega meanwhile dressed in a blue silk robe, Zintgraff's gift to him, an embroidered cotton knitted cap, and long necklace of yellow glass beads. To the right and below him sat 50 to 70 elderly men, his close associates, quietly smoking their pipes. Near the 'sacredpile of stones' sat the musicians. Tita N'yi played a large drum, some beat on dried logs, others blew horns and others played the marimba or calabash-piano. To one side 20 of Garegtfs older wives danced, shaking iron anklets filled with pebbles. To the centre went some of Garegd's office-holders, dancing in fine robes, with long trains trailing behind them.

'Garega called for a pause in the middle of the dance and took me by the hand and followed by his speakers and elders, walked to the pile of stones. Raising my arm he had the silent, sitting crowd informed as follows: 'Look, this white man has come to our country. Do not think that because he is small he is not to be feared. The leopard is small too, but you fear it by day and night. The white man has a good and a bad side, like the moon. He is going to stay with us and we will build for him, so that he likes it here. Whoever harms him or his people, I will kill him'.'

THE STATION

The building of Zintgraff's station took longer than expected, as bamboo (raffia) wood was scarce.

'These bamboo poles had to be carried from groves which were either the property of sub-chiefs or of neighbouring villages. In the last resort hundreds of armed men would remove them, so that the cutting of poles in a particular place is almost a kind of a raid.'

The place Zintgraff chose was a flat-topped ridge to the north of Ball town, and divided from it by a small valley. As neither he nor his carriers knew how to build in bamboo and clay he took little hand in the house-building, but busied himself with making paths and gardens. Fon Garega come each morning to survey the work. In about six weeks 40 huts and a 4-roomed house for Zintgraff were built. This was in spite of the fact that the people were busy harvesting.

Throughout, Zintgraff and his carriers, as well as the builders, were fed by 30 or 40 of Fon Garegd's older wives.

Zintgraff here gives a detailed account of Bali house-building, including the 'prefabrica-ting of the bamboo frames.

'During this time I saw many embassies from distant places who came with gifts to visit me and report on me to their chiefs.'

Garega would not let Zintgraff spend too much time with them and advised him not to make himself cheap.

'With the chiefs from the edge of the Grassneld and my blood-brother Fo Bessong, who was also a trade-friend of Garega's, we have frequent dealings.'

Zintgraff describes his attempt to send a letter to his assistant Zeuner at Barombi by Banyang attending Babessong market. But the Banyang would not let it through. Mean-while on the coast and in Germany it was believed that the expedition had been broken up by the Banyang. In fact he had narrowly escaped an attack. He also learnt that on the way back to Ball 200 warriors from the village which had visited Babessong were proposing to ambush him, but were put off by his 200-strong caravan. [Present day oral tradition suggests that the village in question was Batibo or Aighwi.] Zintgraff also heard a rumour that another white man with a small company was warring in the forest whom Zintgraff thought might be an Englishman. Garega proposed to Zintgraff that if the white man turned up, and was not his brother, they should both attack him and divide the spoils. This disturbed Zintgraff who told Garega that in the circumstances no white man could feel safe. Garega then offered Zintgraff blood-brotherhood, which he accepted very readily. The same ceremony as that adopted by Bessong was undergone.

'The words with which Garega accompanied the ceremony were remarkable: 'You came like a little chicken into my house, white man, and I could have easily killed you and taken your valuables. But since you have been staying with me, I have seen and learnt something of the fashion of the whites. Yet there are many people round me advising me to kill you. But do not fear, for I will not harm you or allow others to harm you, for it is better to obtain the knowledge of the whites and to have them as friends to our lasting benefit, than to take a short-lived advantage of them by robbery".'

The one thing Garega would not permit was a visit by Zintgraff to Bamum where lived a mighty prince with a town so big that a battle at one end of it could not be heard at the other. Garega feared that if Zintgraff went there he would forget Bali and not return.

THE FON AND HIS PEOPLE

Zintgraff then discusses Garega's character—some thought him a kindly, harmless man, others a rogue. He did indeed veer between frankness and arbitrariness based on mistrust, but he was always shrewd and observant, he was not the kind of man a European could lead easily, and dealing with him required tact and care. Zintgraff realised very well that Garega wanted to profit by his visit, but this was natural, and compensated for by the excellent manners of Garega and his court.

'Garega's power over his people is unlimited. Open resistance to commands is nil; more than once I saw the old king break his spear in fury over the bsnt back of some unpunctual sub-chief. But he was very clever at sensing the wishes of the populace, for which he had a kind of senate of 50 or 60 older men in constant session. Nothing was undertaken and no law announced without the certainty that it would be carried out.

ZintgratT's first house in Bali (built February-March 1889)

Where he came up against some passive resistance from a less enlightened section of his entourage, he took what might seem to us a rather unusual way out, namely, a tem-porary resignation and retirement. Seeming tired of the burden of the government he would retire alone to a distant farm, sit down in a retired place and wait there in pique for hours. It often needed many prayers from his followers, who searched for him everywhere, before he would consent to return to his duties and naturally he required unqualified and ready obedience before he agreed to return. His return was consequently a victory march.

Garega has about 200 wives living in a special village in Bali town. Only a few favourites are in his immediate company. As soon as these become pregnant they retire, and make way for younger ones.

While the younger wives look after their lord and master, the elder ones work in the farms, prepare corn meal or cook the food for their husband, servants, wives and children. Garega has not yet had any trouble over new dresses. The ladies of the court, like other Bali women, go about in naked innocence apart from the fact that young women, after the birth of their first child put on a little skirt made out of leaves and grass called guassi: the making and the renewal of this article of clothing is as easy as it is free of expense.

The lands of Garega are extensive and oneoftensees hundreds of men working in them. Zintgraff then refers to Garega's open-handedness with food and drink.

'Garega's eldest sons Tita N'yi and M'bo are the only members of Garega's family to play a prominent part. According to Bali law Tita N'yi, as the eldest, should be his father's heir, but Garega had selected the worthier younger man. For this reason there had been enmity between them till my arrival, and it might have been the reason why, at a later date, Garega wished me to be in command of all Bali and appoint his successor; this, he hoped, would have avoided a bloody civil war at his death.

The whole tribe consists of 6,000 true Bali with 1,500 warriors, and the so-called Bakon-guan dwelling in the sub-towns, about 15,000 with 3,500 warriors, among whom the Barru-nyi are the most numerous. Men bear arms from 14 to 60 years of age. The Bako-nguan living in the northern part of Bali were the original owners of the land and were defeated some 75 years ago by the Bali who made their way here from their homeland in south Adamawa. Since the vanquished were allowed a certain autonomy they accommodated themselves to the new conditions and one can see that in the course of time they have grown together with the Bali. The combined people under the common name of Bali with Garega at their head is the most feared of the inland tribes.'

Zintgraff then says that other Bali groups split off from the invading army and mentions Bali-Kumbat.

Zintgraff describes the physique of the Bali as muscular, above middle height and long-legged, and their bearing proud. The skull is shaped in childhood by gently stroking to an egg shape. The incisor-teeth are usually chipped into points in men; amongst women the upper incisors are knocked out at seven years and only the lower ones are sharpened. The hair is shaved with a triangular razor by both sexes, but sometimes an elliptical comb from forehead to occiput is left, or the front hair shaved only. A specially male style is leaving a small top-knot, which is sometimes plaited and decorated with cowries etc. Camwood is commonly rubbed on by both sexes. Men wear gowns—'togo' or war-shirts— 'n'tchi rrfburri'; women sometimes wear aprons of beads with brass ornaments at big dances. Bali men frequently wear a skull-cap of palm-fibre, often decorated with cocks' feathers. The warriors' feather headresses are chiefly made of black and white feathers. The Bali are never without weapons. On the right hip, from a leather hanger, hang 2 or 3 daggers. From the left shoulder hangs a broad, two-edged cutlass. In the hand is held a dane-gun and spear. These weapons are ornamented or embossed with iron or brass decorations. However, it is forbidden to approach the chief armed. No Bali is seen without a bag, a fibre one or one of civet, antelope or leopard skin, in which his tobacco, ornamented clay pipe, and drinking cup are kept. Some of the notables have brass cups for palmwine, 'rfdu', or maize-beer, 'n'kang.'

'Garega would frequently meet his notables outside the palace in the late afternoons for drinks. The Bali have a day, 'tchun n'tarf', set aside weekly, on this day people go to drink palmwine with the chief or sub-chiefs from 6 a.m. onwards. On these occasions which also have a religious significance, a great deal is discussed and thrashed out. Although weapons are in existence and much excitement obtains, these discussions are kept within bounds.'

BALI LIFE

The daily routine of life is described. Fires burn indoors throughout the cold weather. As soon as housework is done the women go to the fields accompanied by one or two armed men. The men either go to neighbouring markets or tap wine, or sit about smoking. More important men concern themselves with political affairs and gather in the market-place in front of Garega's compound where groups of Bali or visiting strangers are to be found most of the day. In the afternoons the women return with baskets of food and fire-wood and slaves come home with palmwine calabashes slung on sticks. The evening meal is taken at sundown and by 8 o'clock everything is quiet.

'The main crops are guinea corn and maize; their cultivation takes up much land and labour, and, on the estates of Garega or other big men, is carried on by hundreds of people... The surface soil is loosened with hoes and heaped into narrow beds several metres long. When the crop is about three spans high the farm is weeded and then remains uncultivated till harvest. This calls for many hands, male and female; the ears are broken from the stalks and stored in large, specially built granaries. The stalks are later pulled up by the roots, when they have begun to dry, and laid carefully between the furrows as manure for the next crop. Apart from this, and grass burning if that can be so regarded, the Bali do not manure theirfarms as we do, and fallows are frequent... Next to maize and guinea-corn, plantains are their next most important crop; then come the different kinds of yam, and several kinds of cocoyam, beans and other items, a choice of 25 cultivated food plants in all. They have already begun, with the seeds I gave them, to grow radishes, horse-radishes, tomatoes, kidney beans, cabbages and potatoes, and Garega enjoys nibbling a salted horse-radish with his palm wine.'

Goats, sheep and, in special villages, pigs are reared, and poultry is plentiful. Cattle are not generally speaking to be found, though there are some Grassland villages where dwarf cattle are to be found. Dogs are bred not only for the hunt but for sale as meat to the forest peoples. Hunting is usually restricted to the grass-burning season. Elephants and leopards may only be eaten by the Fon and his nobles and are forbidden to subject chiefs.

Ball industry is not highly developed and they buy the goods they need from other Grass-land peoples, e.g. tools, knives etc. These they get from inland peoples whose smiths cani make spears, hoes and bullets from local iron. But the manufacture of tobacco pipes is a Bali speciality.

'In the Bali area a form of currency is in daily use. This is the so-called 'tchang'; or brass rod, of the length of an arm and pencil thin, which is formed into a spiral ring. It is worth the same length of cloth or about 25 pfennig in current coin. It is used forj purchases of slaves, goats, sheep, hens and weapons when these are not exchanged foi cloth, gunpowder or salt. Tchang is frequently buried to hide it from envious eyes. Every kind of ware, with the exception of slaves and ivory is handled in the market..., These are traded privately at night behind closed doors, or in out of the way places.

The Bali... picked up the Bush English and even the vernaculars of the carriers very fast.

Our Bali troops later learnt the German words of command and were, in the opinion; of their training officers, as quick off the mark as our German recruits.

It is difficult to get any insight into Bali religious beliefs as they are reserved and unwilling to talk on the subject. Definite ideas of God and an organised cult are absent. 'There is a belief in spirits which expresses itself in various situations, and angry ghosts, and their appeasement, are in the centre of things.'

There is a belief in the removal of evil influences by sprinkling parts of the body with, water, as in the breaking of blood-friendship. Painting the feet and belly with white clay when partaking of palmwine on 'tchu ritarf is supposed to protect from wounds. Food and drink is provided for angry ghosts when people fall ill. At harvest time the servants swing bull-roarers in each compound and farm to keep away evil influences: they may not be seen by women. Thresholds are protected by small gutters in which a medicine, usually meal, camwood and water, is placed—camwood is rubbed on before all important undertakings. Nikob denotes a superior being, it seems a fearful bush-demon. A good God is not worshipped. Nikob is propitiated when bad things happen. Imported Hausa amulets are worn on the forearm in battle.

Garega himself said it was no good racking one's brains over things which could not.' be seen or heard, but he would accept missionaries as he believed that religious belief would be good for his people, not limiting himself to one denomination, as good things must be taken from all sides.

'In these regions there is a constant state of war, expressed not so much in definite' battles—though these occur—but in frequent ambushes and raids. However the general lack of security has led to the emergence of a genuine national feeling, since small com-j munities have joined together in alliances sanctified by blood-friendship. Even thoug the Bali are mistrustful of one another and seldom trust the word of a foreigner, once blood-friendship has been established they adhere to it scrupulously—this is in contrast to other African peoples for whom it is an empty formality and is regarded as a means of getting presents or other advantages by the chief concerned. But here in the Grassfields it has a kind of sacredness... The form of its consummation varies from place to place... But the mutual drinking of blood of the parties seeking alliance, the 'mixing oil bodies' and the figurative joining of bodies and wills is everywhere its basic feature Garega expressed this in a forceful way by saying 'We have two bellies, but one head'

DEPARTURE

Now that the station farm had been established Zintgraff was ready to continue his expedition. Garega was unwilling to let him go but blood-friendship forbade him the use of force. Nevertheless his warnings made Zintgraff's carriers nervous and disinclined to march. Fon Garega warned Zintgraff that there were many hostile tribes on ths route to Adamawa, and that the Fon of Bafut was outstanding for his cunning and greed: a few years back (i.e. before 1889) he had robbed and murdered some 'white' people (perhaps Fulani) who had settled with him to trade for some five years. He also said that even if they got past Bafut they would face a march across an uninhabited wilderness where they would die of hunger. Moreover, Zintgraff's carriers and headmen had been very well looked after in Ball. The Fon had found them wives and they were richly fed, and they were unwilling to leave Ball. The Fon however agreed to Zintgraff's departure at the end of April. Zintgraff's overseer was dismayed and wanted to wait for the arrival of Zintgraff's assistant Zeuner with reinforcements. But Zintgraff managed to put courage into his followers. Next day a dozen of Fon Garega's oldest councillors visited him to wish him well.

'But they made one request: I must not put Garega, my friend, to shame, by not coming back and building my house elsewhere. I gave them my oath and to make it stronger, we rubbed each other with camwood.'

Soon after, Tita M'bo the second eldest son of Garega came with four wooden rods, said to have been sent by four chiefs allied to Bafut as a sign of war. Zintgraff laughed these to scorn and went on packing. Garega at first ruffled by Zintgraff's contempt, later sent him wine with the message' You have a strong heart; go but come back as you promised.' Next day all was in readiness. Zintgraff however left behind a Lagos headman, 30 men unfit for the march and some captured Banyang women; these were left in the care of Tita M'bo whose large compound lay in the valley below the station on the other side of the stream. Zintgraff marched his men to the 'ntan' to take leave of Garega, and was taken into his private drinking-house where he again promised to return.

Fon Garega gave the order to march himself. Bringing me to the gate of the compound he told me to wait. Some old men appeared and handed him a strangely shaped wand while his servant respectfully brought forward a calabash of clear water and a fresh twig. This Garega dipped in the water, murmured some secret words, and sprinkled the stone threshold, my face and my neck. Then he put his arm round me, and looking once more straight into my eyes, pointed the way and bade me go.'

The caravan left by the north-east gate very quietly. Tita M'bo met them to say farewell and after a last handshake with him, 'the most polished and helpful of all Bali', Zintgraff went on his way.

MANKON AND BAFUT

On the first day, 25th April 1889, they reached Bande (Mankon) passing through a number of small villages more or less tributary to Bah, and breakfasting at Bafutchu. Just before Bande they crossed a large stream, flowing towards the JBenue, and reached the ditch surrounding Bande. Bande was a very big place, 2½ times bigger than Bali and older to judge by the age of the trees. The Fon of Bande was hospitable but reserved partly because of his fear of Bali, even though he had trade-dealings with Tita Nyi, Garega's eldest son, and partly because of his strained relations with Bafut. In another 1½ hours they came within sight of Bafut.

'After one and a half hour's march from Bandeng, the notorious Bafut came in sight and great cries of astonishment over its size arose from the carriers who looked at me with questioning faces. In fact, a town on seven hills in a grove of ancient fig trees lay before us four or five times larger than Bali. On a hill about half an hour away from the town, the expedition halted and camped in a defile. An embassy was sent to the chief asking whether we should come on. Two hours passed before the answer was returned, and then we went forward through a boggy valley and then up the slopes on the top of which lay Bafut.

In the first suburb we were detained by one of the sub-chiefs, who seemed almost autonomous. He brought us goats and palm wine, and was richly rewarded. Here we had to wait for over an hour for the messengers of the chief to fetch us. Finally they appeared, four wide awake fellows in war dress, their scabbards hung with bells which jingled as they walked. From here on we were in their charge and the office of the Bali guides was at an end. We were conducted for at least two hours along an upper snaky path and at four o'clock we stood in a broad market place in the shadow of giant rubber trees, I on one side with my people, on the other numerous armed Bafut. We waited there for a long time watching each other. Then the Bafut rushed forward, fired their dane guns into the air, and held out the butts ia greeting. In return, I had my guides and overseers return the compliment by holding out the butts of their rifles towards the Bafut. Then followed brief questions and answers: Who are you? Where have you come from and where are you going to? After which the Bafut returned to their original positions and were obviously awaiting the formal greeting of the expedition. After setting down the loads, I let my people rush forward and fire three shots which were not without some effect on the onlookers. In a little time, we were led through a maze of buildings but it was not for some time that we were called to the roomy court-yard of the chief. A number of men were already there so that it was hard for us to find room in front of a kind of verandah where the chief was to receive us. The chief of Bafut let me wait in the forecourt for yet another hour, but sent me out the usual little stool which was so small that it hardly accommodated me. My impatience had reached a climax when finally ten slaves ran out of a side door and laid down a large leopard skin on which they set three finely worked stools, and disappeared again. Finally the chief, Gwalem by name, appeared.

He was a plump figure of medium height, clothed in close-fitting mail shirt of blue beads, and a red loin-cloth, some four metres long, which he, so as not to stumble, kicked behind him as he walked. In one hand he held a buffalo horn filled with palm wine, his other hand held up his train against his body. His nose in the air, he stood between two respectful sub-chiefs, the picture of an African despot such as I had not ever seen before or was ever to see again. The people greeted their chief with a threefold clap, as the Balis do.

I arose and went towards the chief, holding out my hand. Perhaps he misunder-stood this movement, perhaps as I thought he was really reaching out his drinking horn to me. In the same moment there arose the sub-chief sitting on the right of the chief to reach for the horn. Seldom have I seen such a passionately angry face as this man bore. The drinking horn was now in my hand, I did not give up, and he asked in a harsh tone 'Who was the chief here?' To which Gwalem ordered him to let the horn be, which he did, but not without giving me a poisonous look. In return I gave him a smile and with a merry 'Prosit!' drank the health of both of them. Then I went back to my seat and set out the object of my journey through the interpreter. Meanwhile Gwalem drank busily, while four old wives with their bodies bent over, their hands before their mouths, stood at his side waiting for his commands. A vessel of food for the carriers, scarcely enough for forty men, and half a dozen calabashes of palm wine were set out, and finally we were led back to a compound which we reached at nightfall.

Next day I found that the chief, in spite of several requests sent us no food. His people too brought hardly anything for sale so that I was forced to open the few sacks of beans that I had brought along as iron rations to stay my people's hunger. Finally, at about 4 p.m. and after Gwalem had asked for the loan of my white teacup, which I never saw again, I was called to see him. He received me in a hall opposite his main house, a fine building made of bamboo with wooden pillars with steps of basalt rock. The hall itself was a long room, open on one side, with a floor tastefully

Some of Garega's elders Nyagan Bandzelin Tita Kuna Fotikale (Unknown) Fontsam (Unknown) Wandiku Fongeam Fogendom. These names were found written in ink or pencil under this plate in Dr P. M. Kaberry's copy of NORD-KAMERUN, which appears to have belonged to the Basel Mission in Bali in 1903. The successors of these notables are still important men in Bali today.

decorated with cowries. On one side of the hall was a sofa-like bed of bamboo covered with leopard skins. The chief lay on this with his drinking horn in his hand. I took my seat on a small but prettily carved stool in the corner... near Gwalem's feet. In the middle of the hall a few logs glowed and a couple of dozen Bafut squatted respectfully before the chief on the ground. My interpreter sat half out of the hall on the open side.'

Zintgraff had the impression that Fon Gwalem was challenging him to a kind of drinking match. 'The people in the hall also got a swig from time to time. Every time that Gwalem belched the courtiers applauded this sign of princely wellbeing. Once the chief started a song which according to the information of one of my Lagos overseers was very like one sung on the Niger, and all sang, in the beat of a march, a sort of round in chorus. I was not to be left out, although I was limited to humming. As night fell, half dozen calabashes were empty, the chief was drunk, and I little better. But the training in holding my liquor I had got in High School served me well. This Gwalem recognised and when I took the lead in the drinking race, he got up on his elbows and looked at me piercingly.'

Zintgraff was still worried by the absence of provisions for his carriers who complained of hunger. Whenever he mentioned the matter he was told to wait, and Zintgraff was worried lest hunger would drive his men to looting. On the next day Zintgraff again had a spree with Fon Gwalem.

'Gwalem had an enormous number of children which I had occasion to observe. A slave appeared with a round-bellied pot filled with cooked beans, swinging a wooden spoon in the left hand. At his call there rushed out of every conceivable corner naked little children of both sexes who surrounded the slave with out-stretched hands.

When I returned to my dwelling I was told that the Bafut had been ordered not to sell food to my people though some had secretly done so for a high price. I was also told that nearby chieflets were coming and going to Gwalem's court. My overseer said to me "You no smell war massa?" And I answered him "Yes, I smell him".'

Zintgraff determined to break out and decided that the best thing to do was to give large gifts to Gwalem and ask him for a guide at the same time. After a long conversation with his retainers in a language unknown to the interpreter, he promised guides next day. Zintgraff then went back and got his expedition ready to depart. He went for a last time to drink with Gwalem.

'There appeared unexpectedly a man with a pot of cooked beans and called my people out of the hall to follow him to some place out of sight to eat. The effect of this was that I was alone with the chief and his entourage. No sooner were my people out of sight than six tall warriors wearing nothing but loin-cloths rushed towards me bran-dishing their knives. Since I was wearing a roomy burnous and was as usual carrying no arms, I was completely helpless while the six fellows with blood-shot eyes waved their knives over my head. The performance lasted long enough for me to realise the hopelessness of any movement. All there remained was to put a good face on it and to die with dignity. Nevertheless, I remembered from my schooldays the story of Pyrrhus and the embassy of Fabricius, and I saw Fon Gwalem from his sofa fasten on me a malicious look. Finally, he called off the fellows with some words I could not understand and they vanished as quickly as they had appeared... A few minutes afterwards my people reappeared.

Gwalem who had perhaps a bad conscience told me through the interpreter to excuse the irruption which was nothing more than the customary fashion of showing respect.

I told the Fon that naturally I had assumed this to be so; but if he thought it necessary for him to excuse himself on the grounds that he frightened me he must be a fool to think that he could worry a white man in this way. And to leave him in no doubt of my meaning, I repeated this to him in Bali. Nevertheless he reached out his horn for me and said that nothing had been further from his mind. So we drank away till nightfall.'

THE MARCH CONTINUES

Zintgraff's expedition was ready to move off at six o'clock next morning, and Zintgraff took the precaution to load all rifles. He met the chief in a private courtyard, who without further formality handed over four guides whose expressions betokened excitement, and unrest.

'The chief said that the way was open and that I could go. My next night camp should be at Babeumka, a town that was even bigger than his. I had nothing to fear. I asked the chief to give strength to his words by mixing blood with me. This he refused to do, but as a sign of his honesty shared with me a kolanut and pepper. I took it but kept my own counsel. Had his attitude been genuine he would have made blood-friendship with me. However I dismissed my Bali guide and went forward.'

Zintgraff was of the opinion that the preparations to ambush him were not ready and put down the outward friendliness of the Bafut and their attempts to delay him to this motive. After he left Bafut, which was visible from the west for three-quarters of an hour from a valley, the road led uphill into mountainous country. But to the north and north-west, this gave way to more lowlying land. He noticed that most of the villages in this area were on hill-tops.

Zintgraff passed by a stream called the Bia (Mentshum or Metcham), which he was told joined a bigger river which led into Bali-Mudi. After crossing this river they came to a little river called Banti, where in spite of Zintgraff's protest, the Bafut guides took provisions by force from the Banti. From there they went along a better path and camped at a little village called Babeka.

Zintgraff's suspicions were aroused by the fact that the villagers were obviously worried, that his guides disappeared and that they were replaced by an old man whom he thought had reached them direct from Bafut in a much shorter time. The new guide led them north-west up the course of the Bia and then suddenly refused to go any further. After the guide's disappearance Zintgraff made a forced march up the valley, but lost his way. Finally after two days' camping, he came to a settled area where the local people were extremely shy, and at length reached a small village built somewhat in the Bali style but much poorer, Bafangu, the capital village of Befa. Here he was met by an embassy from the Babeumka, which lay between Bafut and Befa on the right hand of the Bia, who commanded him curtly to visit their chief. [The largest settlement corresponding to this description is the federated town of Wum or Aghem]. Zintgraff suspected a trap. With the help of the Befa people and their chief he made them drunk, carried on his preparations to leave and slipped away next day on his way, thankful to the honest chief.

He marched up the right bank of the Bia seeing a few villages on the opposite bank. Zintgraff's shoes had worn out by now and he marched barefoot. The river was crossed on a tie-tie bridge and then Zintgraff struck out into uninhabited country for 8 days, 5 without food, until Gani, a sub-town of Takum, was reached. Here they were met by a Takum envoy, the Hausa Landakari, who told them to wait until permission to go forward was received from the ruler of Takum. This came after ten days. Landakari guided the expedition via Big Gani, Burruba andKofi to Takum, a 4 days' journey.

TAKUM AND THE BENUE LANDS

'Takum gave the appearance of a Moslem town. It was surrounded by a mud wall with battlements, bastions and gates, behind which could be seen the pointed roofs of houses, leafy shade-trees and the feathery tops of Carica papaya. At its gate stood the elders of the town in colourful silk robes; all wore yellow or red leather slippers. For the first time I was ashamed of my ragged appearance, and particularly of my bare feet. However the elders were very courteous and after my interpreter had introduced me as a friend of Flegel's they led us without more ado into the big town. In the wide market-place there sat under a wide-spreading shady tree – for it was just after midday – the paramount chief of the Takum – district – the sultan Yakubu. Yakubu, a fine figure of a man not unlike the Bali fon in appearance, but much darker, expressed his astonishment over our coming by the route we had, which we had only managed with God's help.'

Zintgraff and his followers camped outside the town. Though grain was short, their hunger was relieved by the sultan's gift of an ox and two sheep. Next morning he was woken by a band of four long tin trumpets and two drums sent by the sultan gave a house in the town. He was still in some difficulty over food as his barter-goods were running low and his 'small change' — sewing-needles — had little value here. The houses were round, thatched huts in Adamawa style and the verandahs were decorated with empty whisky and brandy bottles, a sure sign of the nearness of a European trading.

On the 5th day of his stay in Takum, Zintgraff was called to the audience where excellent palm wine was put before him. Here were Yakubu's chief minister, the galadima, some notables, and Yakubu's favourite horse.

'In my conversation with Yakubu I found confirmation of Fon Garega's story that the Bali had come from these northern regions. Yakubu showed us an ancient loin-cloth of native cotton, such as is part of the Bali national dress and worn under the gown wi the ends trailing on the ground. Yakubu also imitated the sound of Garega's ivory trumpets, and repeated the greeting of the Bali — 'O la n'di, fon' — very correctly, finally he explained that Garega's father and his own father were cousins, and that the first Garega (Garega's father?) had retired to the Bali uplands to get away from Fulani slave-raids, and had conquered all the tribes in his path. The Bali called Adamawa 'n'gong Puri', land of the FulanL Yakubu asked many searching questions about Garega's present situation and seemed pleased that I was Garega's blood-friend.'

Zintgraff contrasts Yakubu' s behaviour with that of other chiefs. Perceiving Zintgraff's poverty he had not asked for gifts. But Zintgraff gave him a revolver and buli^c return received a fine saddled horse. They parted excellent friends.

On 28th May, 1889, Zintgraff reached Donga, where he found it simpler to take on the same name as that used by Flegel in these parts — Abder-Rahman. He was well received by the people who wanted a counterpoise to the Royal Niger Company's unpopular monopoly.

He was received in audience by the sultan of Donga and, remembering Fon Garega's advice that 'clothes make the man' wore a white silk gown from Lagos and turban. During his stay he witnessed the 'Moslem Christmas' and notes that the sultan's body-guard wore a uniform of cloth imitating leopardskin, and black goatskin helmets with red chinstraps.

After a five-day stay in Donga he left for Okari (Wukari). He gave 25 flints to the sultan and received in return a tusk of 20 kilos. In Okari clean out of trade goods, but two chests of provisions and a letter appeared addressed 'to the European said to be at Donga' from Mr Macintosh, agent of the Royal Niger Co., who invited him to Ibi.

Next day Zintgraff reached Ibi, and approached Macintosh's house, led by an astonished African clerk. Here he was heartily welcomed and his carriers given quarters. He stayed at Ibi as the Company's guest for four days. He notified his arrival at the Benue to Berlin by telegraph. The temptation to return to Duala or Europe by river-steamer to the Niger mouth and then by coast-wise steamer was great. He was held by his promise to Garega to return. This he could have done via Duala. But he decided that the moral effect of his first passage could best be maintained by coming down again to the coast if possible in company with some Bali. Moreover, he wished to visit 'German' Adamawa and return to Bali via Banyo if possible.

This was approved by the German Government.

Zintgraff had opportunity to compare the Royal Niger Company with German firms. He notes that the Britons were educated men and gentlemen, and that the Company felt it worth while to recruit outstanding men as agents.

THE RETURN THROUGH ADAMAWA

Zintgraff now set out for Banyo, staying at Songos en route, noticing the bodies of slave-carriers and donkeys along the route left heartlessly to die by their masters. His heart was wrung by an old slave carrying marks of whippings on his back and he would have liked to have bought and freed him, but the old man could not have kept up with Zintgraff's rapid march, Zintgraff met several caravans bringing slaves, ivory and other goods. These slaves were not very brutally treated and few carried loads, but they were kept under armed guard and weak and hungry so that they could not run away. The ones who collapsed were left to die and were eaten by vultures. These sights convinced Zintgraff that European rule had some moral justification, Zintgraff went via Mala Mala to Bakundi where he stayed eight days to recover from his exertions. Here there was a Royal Niger Co. factory, under an efficient Sierra Leonean, Mr Lewis, who was most helpful.

At Bakundi he met FlegeVs friend and guide Madugu Gaschi M'Baki, who, together with Madugu ban Tambari, had stayed in Berlin with Mr and Mrs Butow. Mr Butow, Treasurer of the Berlin Geographical Society, acted as 'father' to all African explorers. Zintgraff asked Madugu to come with him to Banyo. Together they then travelled towards Gashaka, Madugu accompanied by one of his wives and a slave who acted as horse-boy.

Gashaka was reached in ten days, staying mostly in Songos. The only town stayed in was Belli. He met the Chief of Belli en route in embarassing circumstances as he was battling with an attack of diarrhoea!

It was the custom in Adamawa for caravans to pay a toll at each town, but Zintgraff refused to pay until he had visited the Chief. This paid off in Gashaka, as its ruler, Sambo, provided excellent hospitality. A cow andcorn was provided for his carriers and ten ladies of the court attended to Zintgraff's wants. A variety of provisions was obtainable in the market.

Adamawa was divided into a number of chiefdoms under the emir of Yola, which, under the Anglo-German agreement lay in the British sphere of interest. But some of the more important chiefdoms—Gashaka, Koncha, Laro, Buba N'Jidda, Ngaundere, Tibati and Banyo for example— lay in the German sphere. These were dependent on Yola for all important matters and sent yearly to Yola a tribute of slaves and ivory which was in turn passed on to the Sultan of Sokoto. This tribute was obtained by regular raids on the surrounding pagans, undertaken almost every year, and they established war-camps—'sanserni'—in the pagan lands.

When Zintgraff arrived in Gashaka in June 75£, the British were making great efforts to bring the emir of Yola under their influence, without much success. Consequently the emir of Yola was suspicious of foreigners, while the Hausa had determined to prevent the entry of European trade and in particular to bar them from the regions from which slaves and ivory came. These were, in particular, the regions which lay in an arc around the southern chiefdoms of Gashaka, Banyo and Tibati, and east of Ngaoundere, part of which Zintgraff had skirted and through which he wished to return to Bali.

Sambo refused to let him travel to Sanyo and turn south there, and told him that permis-sion to go there could only be obtained from Yola. Zintgraff was forced to agree and set out for Yola with 25 Liberian boys and a guide, Yakada, on 15th July, 1889.

Zintgraff made the 520 km. journey to Yola, via Laro and Koncha, in fourteen days. The route was not by any means safe, because of the raids of rebellious tribes. Some three days out from Yola he came upon an empty camp-site and evidence of its recent sack. Here they were joined by some frightened Hausa traders.

There were numerous Hausa and Fulani settlers to be seen, the latter with large herds. The ruling house of Adamawa was of Fulani stock, but the Fulani had become economically dependent on the Hausa. Zintgraff wondered whether Europeans could ever compete successfully with them. The Hausa traders had acted as spies and scouts for the Fulani, pointing out new slaving-grounds to them, and the Fulani had followed behind. The Hausa markets were to be found in every Adamawa town: here slaves from the south were ex-changed for fine cloth from Timbuctoo, ivory for English and Indian cottons, kolas for Hausa cloth. Here also Hausa leather and metalwork were sold. Zintgraff stayed only two days in Yola: he was politely received but firmly told that he could not go to Sanyo.

He was much pestered by visitors seeking free gifts. Yola, a town of 15,000 people, was smaller in extent than Bafut. The emir very kindly refused Zintgraff's gift until his request could be discussed, and explained to Zintgraff that it could not be granted as the southern vassals were rebellious.

Zintgraff tried to overawe him with tales of German power and promises of German friendship against the English, but he could not say whether his words were translated by Madugu. The English were unpopular at any rate since one of their agents had insulted some noblewomen. The then emir, Sonda (Sanda) died soon after and his successor opened Yola to trade without discrimination. Zintgraff returned to Gashaka on 15th August, 1889. He found his carriers had got little food in his absence but they had earned their keep by selling firewood.

Sambo invited Zintgraff to stay with him over the rainy season and accompany him in a war in the Sanyo direction. But Zintgraff felt that it would be morally wrong for a Euro-pean to be present at a slave-raid. So he bade Sambo farewell and Sambo gave him a guide to take him back to Takum via Ashaku. Even though Sambo was a slave-raider, he had his generous side. Zintgraff gave him a Swiss Vetterli rifle. Madugu left him on the way to Takum.

The journey from Gashaka to Takum took 14 days and went along the line up to which the slave-raiders had advanced. They passed through Dorro, whose chief sent tribute of slaves and ivory to Gashaka and arrived at the independent village of Bussum, where their arrival caused fear and excitement among its inhabitants, armed with bows and arrows, as well as spear and shield. They camped outside the village, and after a false alarm of raiders, made friends with the villagers.

Ashaku, 3 hours west of Bussum was the most southerly settlement of Hausa. After a day there, they attempted to cross the Donga River. They met a small Hausa caravan, floating their goods across the river in huge gourds and swimming after them. They got their loads across with the help of a raft. No more villages were met, though a few on the southern hills were seen, and their passage was marked by drum-signals. Four days from Ashaku near Gegea, a large deserted raiding camp of the Sultan of Donga was seen. On the eighth day they reached Tissa, crossing the Donga again by canoe. They could get no guide here, but next day hit a path which led them to the Takum plain over a range of hills. Riders came out to meet them and Yakubu greeted them joyfully.

TAKUM, BUM, BIKOM

From Takum Zintgraff had intended to return to Bafut, because he had said he would, and because he did not wish to give the impression that he feared to do so. Yakubu agreed to help him but owing to a misunderstanding—Zintgraff's belief that Bafut and Bafum (Bum) were the same—he returned a different way. There were a few Bafum people in Takum and these looked like Bafuts. In Takum he found a Lagos man who had deserted in Ibi. Yakubu interceded for him so he was not severely punished. He met yet another Lagos man, a trader who had been to Bornu and then Yola and had arrived in Takum after his caravan had been robbed. Yakubu gave his villages orders that Zintgraff's expedition were to be provided with maize as they were going through uninhabited country but there was little to be had. The route was so rough and fodder so hard to get that Zintgraff sent back his horse 'Takum' to Yakubu by a passing caravan. Two days from Takum the Katsina Allah river was crossed in spite of the unwillingness of the people on the left bank to lend a canoe. All around could be heard flutes, used here as signals. Leaving these villages behind they entered into a country side deserted by its peoples because of slave-raids.

On the way Zintgraff stayed in a camp—Songo Nasara—undoubtably established by the Takum chief as a raiding centre. On the third day out they met a Hausa caravan coming from Bafum (Bum) of about 50 people, heavily laden with ivory and kolas.

'The village reached was Guanasse where we met some Hausa.' Here their Takum guide left them. They camped among reeds, and were told that the Bafum chief would greet them next day in the capital. The country was well cultivated. The villages were mostly near streams, and the kola tree seemed to be intentionally cultivated. The numerous Bafum, armed with spears, seemed at first astonished at their coming, but seemed good natured and started bargaining with them. Here a Ball speaker was found, a man who had run away from Ball to Bafut, and had been sold from Bafut to Bafum. His name was Fon, and Zintgraff begged his services from the Bafum chief.

Two of Zintgraff's people died of exhaustion, but he was not allowed to bury them by the local people. Zintgraff now reached very hilly country and two days out from Bafum reached Deng (Achan ?) whose numerous inhabitants were very hospitable. Here Zintgraff entered the region of charcoal-burning and iron industry. The smoke from charcoal-making could be seen rising from woody hills to the south.

The country became more difficult, and two more men died of exhaustion. On the third day they came to the valley leading south-east which its inhabitants called 'Bekom' (Bikom) and camped in empty huts. No conversation was possible with the inhabitants until an old man in a Ball gown was met: he offered to act as guide.

In the last third of the valley they heard elephant horns and were suddenly surrounded by warriors who were only pacified with difficulty with the help of the old man. ft seemed that thechief was piqued that Zintgraff had not asked permission to enter and wanted to seehim. The Bekom seemed very excitable. The war-party was led by four young men, princes perhaps, with war-shirts, feather caps, decorated powder horns, spears and dane-guns. In spite of Zintgraff's request no food was brought.

On the third day of waiting Zintgraff learnt that twelve of his men had been imprisoned. Zintgraff finally got them released after threatening to fight, but all their goods had been stolen. Apologies were made, but Zintgraff replied that his anger would only be stilled if provisions were brought. At last some provisions came, and generous payment was made for them, including a tin trunk for the chief. Zintgraff also demonstrated his carbine to the Bekom, with some effect.

Zintgraff decided to march next day, but missing his way, was overtaken by the princes who told him their father, the Chief, was coming. But Zintgraff would not wait; he was, however, given a spear as a passport through the land. After three hours forced march they reached the edge of the plateau and looked down on a broad, fertile, plain, watered by a large river (the Ndop Plain). They hit a path leading down to a large village. Zintgraff sent out some messengers to the village who returned in two hours to say that the village was friendly, but that Bekom, recognisable by their green parrot-feather caps, were present. However messengers from the chief soon came with a pressing invitation to stay, but Zintgraff thought it wiser to put a larger distance between him and the Bekom. They marched some way by compass.

E. M. Chilver

BAMUNGU (BABUNGO)

'While I was trying to cross a brook, a message came from the rear that natives without weapons were following us. I was wondering what to do when a messenger of the chief, a stately man with an attractive face, suddenly stood before me. As a sign of peace, he carried a woman's spear, and asked us at least to wait until the chief himself came. The chief soon appeared, accompanied by his ten unarmed men. A cowhide was stretched, a stool set out, and he sat down looking at me keenly, while the crowding carriers looked on. He, Fo Mungu was his name, made a very good impression with his full-bearded homely face. He asked through one of his servants why we did not wish to visit him, and whether we thought him a dangerous man. He had nothing to do with Bekom. We should pay him the honour of coming, and staying a few days with him, and he would certainly take us to Bali. We should have plenty to eat and drink, so much so that we would have some left over to give the messengers. This invitation made a great impression on the empty stomachs of our people. When I asked Baitabe (my overseer) his opinion, he said, grounding his rifle—' Well masta we go for town; if them want fight, we fight them; them no fit kill we like fowl'. And so we turned about after firing a greeting shot for the chief.

Half way we met an embassy from Bekom which had hurried after us, bringing two goats and a calabash of palmwine which had broken on the way.

The village of Fo Mungu (Babungo) is the prettiest of all the Grassland villages which I have seen, and the well kept, well cleaned fields put all others into the shade. At the entrance to it, we saw some stragglers from our party already busy with the preparation of food provided by the villagers. In front of every house, banana leaves were laid out like tablecloths on the ground, on which cooked cocoyam dumplings, maize and porridge for the refreshment of our carriers had been laid out. These soon made short work of the food, but a greater surprise awaited us when we reached the large market place lined with its old shady trees. Thousands of natives had collected here—on one side the women with numerous children and babies, on the other, men and boys. All were without weapons and looking on in respectful silence. The chief halted, and spoke thus to his people. 'Look at him my people, this is the white man who is like God. I have brought him so that he can see you and the village. Behave well to him and his people so that he feels well in our village, and forgets the bad things he has experienced on his way'. After these loudly spoken words, the silence broke and, as the chief took me by the hand, we walked together while loud cries of joy were raised, and the nearby men made way for me and brushed away the dust from before us. We had to walk carefully so as not to tread on any of these good people, and the chief had some difficulty in holding back the press of people, particularly the women and children, with his horse-tail switch.

I was the first white man to be seen by these people and they, so far off from civilization, had thrown themselves at my feet in a simple enthusiasm, which was not either curiosity or greed but a better, more honest, sentiment of pious reverence, springing from the belief that the white man was a different kind of being whose appearance could only portend luck and peace. I felt unexpectedly a sort of shame, a sort of Faust feeling.

I stayed three days with Fo Mungu and could bear witness to the outstanding peace-ableness of this tribe, which seemed to enjoy great respect not only because of its large population but because of the wisdom of its chief. In the matter of manners and morals Fo Mungu is far superior to the Bali chief Garega, whose hospitality is generally tinged with calculation. By contrast Fo Mungu said 'I and my people are good; so the white man who is also good, will feel well amongst us.'

The Bamungu are outstanding ironsmiths. The smith's craft is respected and the chief selects from amongst them his confidential servants. The Bamungu swords, knives and hoes are distributed widely through the country. A sword with which Fo Mungu honoured me has the exact form of a Roman gladius and was faultlessly made. I also saw at his place one of those small kettle-like vessels of copper which Moslems use for their ablutions. From here Banyo could be reached without great difficulty and he would have been prepared to help me. The embassies of the big chiefs living on the route to Banyo, e.g. Bangola, gave me the impression that they were well disposed. I also learned that Fo Mungu was a trade friend of Garega's second son, M'bo, and as a sign of this Fo Mungu showed me a piece of camwood which he had received as a gift from him a few days earlier. As regards provisions for my carriers, Fo Mungu literally kept the promise he had given at our first meeting, and I was extremely sorry that I could only reward his generous hospitality so meanly. On the third day he gave us guides and we marched from the low lying land round Bamungu into the heights.'

TO BALI VIA BAMBUI AND BAFRENG

As they reached the top of the mountain, the weather suddenly worsened and they met with icy cold and hail storms. Zintgraff's carriers could not stand it and some lay down to die; he did his best to keep them moving, but even he, used to the cold, was stiff in the joints. When he reached Bambui, whose chief sheltered and entertained them, he learnt to his sorrow that a number of carriers had died of exposure.

Next day they reached Bafuen (Bafreng), a kind of Bali vassal, and were well received. Then they marched through the subject towns of Munda (Menda Nkwe—Bamendd) and Ngoa, where refreshments awaited them. On the outskirts of Bali town they were met by the Tita M'bo and his people bringing food and wine.

They marched through the town in orderly ranks, while horns and drums sounded, to the market-place. Here Garega sat like a bronze statue on his stone throne. He gave Zintgraff a meaning-laden look and then sprang up and embraced him. The next few days passed in celebrations and story-telling while palm wine flowed like water. The station then had to be restored and improved as Zintgraff intended it to be the future centre of government in the region.

He had few trade-goods left but Garega saw to his carriers by quartering them in different compounds. Zintgraff's prisoners were released on paying a ransom which he gave to his followers. But trouble was to come from the death, above Bambui, of the Banyang princess, MiyimbVs daughter. Zintgraff tried to make peace with the Banyang but they refused it. According to Fo Bessong they believed that they had deprived Zintgraff of power by capturing his accordion, around which they had built a shrine.

RETURN TO THE COAST

Six weeks passed. On the 24th December 1889, Zintgraff began his march to the coast. He left behind seven Vai-boys, our as a punishment for pilfering. Garega gave him eleven men, three older men and eight younger fellows, and had him escorted some 25 km. by a force of 1,500 men, who were going to punish a village for robbing Fo Bessong. Fo Bessong greeted Zintgraff joyfully and gave him provisions. The expedition marched so rapidly that the Banyang hardly had time to gather. They tried an ambush just beyond Fo Tabe's but were repulsed with ease.

The appearance of the Ball caused great excitement among the slave-villages peopled by Grassfielders but their masters were taken aback. Without much difficulty they reached Barombi Station, now empty since Lt. Zeuner had fallen ill and returned to Europe. An agent of the firm Jantzen and Thormahlen, which had opened a factory at Mundame was there and helped to establish local trade contacts. On 5th January, 1891, he entered Duala with his advance party, including his Bali companions.

Zintgraff then travelled with the Governor, von Soden, to San Thome to report his story in full. It became clear that, had anything gone amiss, he could not have been rescued as the Governor had no resources to spare: nevertheless worried by his long absence the Governor had sent two small expeditions to get news. News had finally come from Nigeria of his break-through, and nine Vai-boys sent back from Ibi had given a partial account of his travels.

The Bali were put in Government quarters, while Zintgraff went on leave to San Thome and Europe. Meanwhile, Zeuner had returned from Europe, and went up with 70 Vai-boys to Barombi to await Zintgraff's return.

REPORT TO GERMANY

Back in Germany, Zintgraff presented a Memorandum to the Colonial Bureau of the German Foreign Office. In this he argued that the Bali lands—he meantbythis the western Grassfields so far known to explorers—should be developed for German trade, as a market for German exports, and as a recruiting area for soldiers and labourers. He believed that large quantities of ivory, at lower prices than to be found elsewhere, lay stored away and that this ivory was finding its way to the Benue and Niger factories and to Calabar through Hausa traders: almost none was getting to Duala. These three outlets were also the distributing points for European goods in the area. The route to Duala was hardly longer than that to Calabar, and it should be German policy to make it open and safe. He also pointed out that a large part, possibly the greater part of the palm-oil and other oil-products originated in the hinterland of the German Protectorate. Zintgraff hoped with Garega's help to recruit his subjects as plantation labourers and soldiers in the Government service. Zintgraff pointed out that a military force was necessary if only for police purposes.

The English had trained Hausa soldiers, the French the Tirailleurs Indigenes (Algerian riflemen) and Laptots (Senegalese). Attempts to recruit Hausa would fail because of English objections. Sudanese soldiers were being tried out but it was doubtful whether they would stand the damp climate, and in any event their recruitment depended on English goodwill; and their transportation and maintenance was expensive. For the plantations also the Germans depended on foreign labour, from the regions around Accra and Monrovia. These sources might easily dry up and anyway recruitment was difficult and expensive, since foreign labourers seldom stayed more than two years. It was worth trying to train the Grass-fielders especially the Bali: they were wild uncivilized people given to raiding and plundering but they had many good characteristics, were intelligent, educable and brave and were united under a really effective paramount chief.

One of the difficulties faced by the German authorities in Kamerun was the division of the people into tiny tribes under little chiefs without much authority, indeed none that the Germans could rely on or was worth their support. Garega was an entirely different case.

'Garega had the intention, no less, of making himself leader of all the Grassfield people. This certainly would be difficult if he were to rely solely on the guns and spears of his 5,000 Bali warriors. He has, indeed, already made a name for himself as a successful warrior and is feared. The Bali had entered the land as conquerors and had continued to expand after their settlement. Then a white man, the first of a race about whose power and wealth many rumours had reached the area, had come to him. Garega had not killed and robbed him but had sought to win his friendship, admittedly in his own interests and possibly over-estimating his power to help. But Garega also saw beyond this, and had found in the European outlook something worthy of respect. 'War and force', Garega used to say, 'make people fear and empties the land, but land without it people is like a burnt-out-fire'. Consequently Garega is aiming to become the chief arbitrator of disputes between the neighbouring tribes. This he sees as the best means of uniting the Grassfields under Bali leadership. Consequently he looks to European support to back up his influence and remove any doubt as to the enforceability and certainty of his arbitration. These and similar thoughts were seldom expressed openly to me by the old king, but occasional remarks made his plans apparent. In order to make the man, his power and his efforts serviceable to our colonial interests, I proposed in my programme the establishment of a Commissionership in Bali to which would be entrusted, as a main preoccupation, the regulation of Garega's leadership and the establishment of a general administration for the Grassfields. The section in question in the Memorandum runs as follows:

'As the situation in the coastal areas now stands, no trader will undertake to penetrate the interior without strong protection or safe roads, nor are the inland tribes inclined on balance for fear of unknown enemies, to come down to the coast withoxit some security, It is desirable, on both grounds to open a route from Mundame to Bali: I regard the river-route from Duala to Mundame as open. It is desirable to establish a Commis-sion at Bali with the following aims:

(i) Protection of European traders, missionaries or other types of incomers;
(ii) Security of the caravan route;
(iii) Justice among the natives and
(iv) Unification of the divided tribes under Garega.

Garega is indeed an African barbarian, honest when it suits him—as in his dealings with the whites, and a bandit when honesty does not suit his purpose, but he has worked out for himself the notion that all should be one—me me i-in. This unity, he believes, can be brought about by the whites, before whom he has already appeared and behaved as a paramount, and he willingly lets himself be thought of as a great king of the future. For him the white man's role is to settle quarrels and put down kidnapping and slave-raiding.

One could harbour doubts as to whether Garega would remain a loyal ally. So far as this is concerned, on my first visit to Bali he was loyal and responsible even in trifling matters. Provided we support and intelligently favour his plans, which are at least in full agreement with ours, it would not be too difficult to bind him lastingly to our inte-rests. This link of common interest would be greatly strengthened by the establishment of a trading station in Bali, the dearest wish of every native chief. With the agreement of the Foreign Office, I set about winning over German traders to this undertaking. It was the Hamburg firm of Jantzen, Thormahlen and Dollmann which agreed to the preparation of a trading expedition to these regions and the establishment of a factory in Bali'.'

E. M. Chilver

A NEW EXPEDITION

At the beginning of 1890 the Governor issued a decree giving monopoly rights to undertakings dealing in or cultivating new products or establishing a station in a new area, for up to ten years. This decree was meant to arouse the interest of German firms in new areas, prevent foreign competition, and recompense the firms for the costliness and danger of pioneering new areas. The foreign Office decided to send out a new expedition, which was to be combined with a trading expedition, and gave Zintgraff a Commission to act on its behalf in the northern districts. In a letter to the Hamburg firm dated 11th August, 1890, it was made clear that Zintgraff was to be in control of all political and military matters affecting both expeditions.

At this time Governor von Soden, after five years in office, resigned on health grounds. He had been a keen supporter of Zintgraff's plans, while the new Governor (Zimmerer) could not view them with the same understanding and goodwill.

Zintgraff's plans suffered another setback when his colleague Zeuner, an outstanding scientist as well as explorer, died of blackwater fever in April 1890, It was difficult to replace him. His deputy at Barombi, Dr Preuss, was primarily a naturalist and had other aims. The choice fell upon Lt. von Spangenberg of the 73rd Infantry, an experienced surveys man. who put some of his own funds at the expedition's disposal; and he was joined by the agriculturist Huwe who was selected as manager of the expedition. Such was the position at 1st September, 1890, when Zintgraff'returned to Kamerun. Zintgraff's terms of reference were as follows:

1. To cement friendly relations with the chiefs;
2. To maintain peace and order in the hinterland;

3. To use all efforts to open undisturbed and secure caravan routes to the coast and back;
4. To channel the trade of the hinterland along these routes to the Kamerun coast.

RETURN TO BALI

As the combined expeditions were to be heavily laden with goods, Zintgraff had to go to Monrovia to recruit some 400 carriers. Here he was opposed by a local German trader, but with the help of his old overseer, Bai Tabe, he managed to collect 300 men there and 70 others in Kamerun. The staff of the trade expedition was as follows: Nehber, leader of the expedition, local agent of Jantzen and Thormahlen and manager of its concerns at Bibundi, and a university graduate; Carstensen, a servant of von Soden's and old soldier with previous exploring experience in Persia; and two caravan leaders, Caulwell, with North African experience and Tiedt, a seasoned sailor. Of the Europeans taking part only Zintgraff and Carstensen returned alive. 200 carriers were assigned to the trade expedition and 175 to Zintgraff; these were divided into groups of 30 under overseers. To his subordinates Zintgraff gave the utmost freedom of action but insisted that no Punishments should be administered without his permission. Both parties met at Barombi which was developed as a rear-station for the expedition and laid out with provision gardens. Before the expedition started von Spangenberg was sent to the Banyang border to make friendly overtures to the Banyang, and if these proved hostile, to lay down provisions with the friendly Chief N'Guti. He returned with the news that Difang now wanted peace and would clean the road to a width of 3 metres. The expedition started out at the end of November,

1890, in small groups of 20 so as not to overburden the villages supplying food. Zintgraff brought up the rear with his 11 Bali men who acted as his bodyguard. They reached N'Guti's without incident. Here the expedition was mustered and some carriers who had beaten up local people were punished. On the 4th December, 1890, Banyang country was now reached. The route, previously populated, was now deserted, and only ruined huts were to be seen. Difang after excuses about his health, finally appeared and Zintgraff read him a lecture to which the Bali 'added some pepper.' Difang led them to Fo Tabe's where Miyimbi was also present and Zintgraff mixed his blood with them as a sign of peace. In return for their food, the expedition gave them an elephant they had killed. Miyimbi was pleased to see one of his daughters again but could not really believe that Zintgraff had not bewitched the daughter who died at Bambui and explained that this was the cause of the previous attack made on Zintgraff on his return-journey. Zintgraff was glad to conclude peace with the Banyang as he was no believer in cheap victories over natives, and thought their effect was temporary and often deplorable. On 9th December, 1890, the expedition entered Bali. There was great excitement and Garega was delighted that Zintgraff had kept his second promise to return. The station had been neglected by the Vai-boys left behind and the Bali people brought in thousands of bamboos for repair and the erection of new buildings. Zintgraff, previously known as Fon M'bang, 'red chief' was now given the nick-name Fon M'borr Ngong, 'chief who strengthens the people.'

Fon Garega felt that his dead father should share in his pleasure and should not be without knowledge of his white visitors and their gifts; so the paternal grave was opened and Garega deposited in it apart of the cloth presented by the expedition.

BAFUT AND MANKON

Garega encouraged the trading expedition to start trade in the whole area. The main sources of ivory lay outside Bali. Almost every day embassies came in, for example from Babungo and from Garega's brother Chief Fon N'soa who lived near the Liba river. These brought fine gifts, for example stock, and went away richly rewarded to spread the news. Some tusks were brought in to test the market. If the price asked was lower than on the coast—1 mark per lb. rather than 4-7 marks—it was nevertheless 100 % higher than the normal Bali market price. In order to test Garega's statement that trade should be opened it was decided to make an expedition to Bande (Mankon) and Bafut, where there was plenty of ivory. Von Spangenberg was detailed to accompany Nehber.

These two set out with 60 Vai-boys on 26th December, 1890. The day before two Vai-boys who had learnt Eali were sent with two of Garega's people to warn the Chiefs of their coming. On 28th December, a despatch came from Nehber with the astonishing news that the Chief of Bande had informed him that the two Vai-boys had been killed by Fon Gualem's orders, but that the two Bali men had been allowed to return. Nehber asked for reinforcements and 200 men were sent under Carstensen andffuwe to Bande to bring him home. An embassy under Zintgraff's servant Isaac had not yet returned from Babungo. It was impossible to discover the exact grounds for the Bafut action. Since the two Bali men had been let go, it seemed to Zintgraff that Gualem had acted on his own impulse; nothing indicated a Bali plot and consequently the apparent friendliness of Bande was doubtful. Next day a conference took place with Garega, in the presence of his confidential servants Fonte and Tituat (Tituwon) and the two messengers who were dependents of Tita M'bo who had trade relations with Bafut.

When Zintgraff said that the murders must be avenged, Fon Garega spoke as follows:

> "White man, I the Fon of Bali, will avenge your servants. Wait until the time comes and you, my blood-friend, will see what I will do for you. Your friends are my friends, your foes are my foes".
>
> 'I [Zintgraff] expected nothing else. After this, I was even more certain of my affairs and knowing that Garega was behind me as a loyal friend, I began negotiations with Bafut, hoping that I could settle the matter in the customary way by the payment of compensation. I was strengthened in this belief by the circumstance that our inquiries showed that the instigator of the murders was the Fon of Bande himself.'

On his past visit, Zintgraff had remarked that the relations between Bafut and Bande were tense. Before his arrival there had been negotiations between Bafut and Bali to combine against Bande. After Zintgraff's return from Adamawa he had demanded a return gift for his own gift, from Bafut, since Bafut had not, as promised, shown him the route. Bafut had sent one ox, which Zintgraff had returned as insufficient since the goods he had given the Fon of Bafut were worth at least 30 oxen, or 150 marks. So matters stood when Zintgraff left Bali for Europe. Zintgraff had now returned with a stronger force. The Fon of Bande, who had not forgotten the dangers of a Bali-Bafut alliance, and informed of the bad relations between Zintgraff and Bafut, tried to curry favour with Bafut by warning him of the dangers of Zintgraff's presence, told him that Zintgraff's Vai messengers were coming to put down bad magic that would weaken him in war, and that Zintgraff himself was coming with an army to fetch his return-gift. Bafut had not killed the Bah messengers because he hoped one day to join Bah in plundering the whites.

Zintgraff reported the affair to the Governor and warned him that hostilities might break out. He asked for reserves of ammunition at Baromb to be brought up to Ball or to the Banyang three day's south of Bah, on the ground that insufficient ammunition made the outcome of a fight somewhat doubtful. In the belief that this would be done, he did not send carriers to Barombi, not wanting to weaken his force. Zintgraff had not realised that the new Governor, Zimmerer, had a different policy from von Soden's and wanted to rely on the coastal people, leaving the inland trade in their hands. Meanwhile Zintgraff's negotiations had failed, Bafut and Bande became open allies and Isaac had only returned with difficulty from Babungo, just avoiding Bafut attacks. Something had to be done if German prestige was not to disappear.

The Bafut and Bande sent magicians to put down magic on the roads to render their foes weak. Zintgraff sent young Bali boys to relieve themselves on these magical objects, a measure which filled Garega with merriment and maintained morale.

After the demand made to Bafut and Bande for compensation of 10 ivories and 5 oxen for the murders had been refused with the reply 'if you are men, come and fetch them yourself, Garega held a war-council, and also called in his priests, magicians and diviners and some old women to make war-magic. Zintgraff meanwhile told his carriers how matters stood. They had not been recruited as soldiers, but soon agreed to fight for a pay-increase while fighting lasted. The 31st January, 1891 was fixed for the fight. On 28th January the Vai-boys were divided into sections. All the Europeans joined in except for Carstensen and Caulwell who were ill with fever. There were about 8 vassal villages lying between Bali and Bande and it was in one of these, Bangwa, that it was decided to assemble. Garega, a feared warrior in his youth, could not take part because of his age, much to his disgust, but handed over the command to Zintgraff in the presence of his two eldest sons and his sub-chiefs.

THE BATTLE OF MANKON

The force set out at midday, 30th January. At the head were a company of scouts, according to native custom, then 100 Bali warriors and behind these the flag-bearer of Garega—not carrying the white Bali flag but the German tricolour presented by Zintgraff. Behind the flag came the five Europeans with 300 Vai, and bringing up the rear-guard about 2,000 Bali with done-guns and spears. They marched in Indian file so as to cover their tracks. Some women came with provisions and Garega's daughter Kossa came with a gun.

The first vassal town reached was Bambutu; here some vassals joined. The true Bali passed in squads of 100-150, recognizable by their plumes, and floating war-shirts of white, red or blue. The combined Bali host was led by Tita N'yi and Tita M'bo. They were followed by Bakonguan allies under their own leaders, less well dressed, but fierce, strong fellows. The allies from the west of Bande were expected that evening. At 2 a.m. Zintgraff's party went forward with the scouts to take their position on a cross-road towards Bande. These scouts, about 40 in Bali, were a remarkable institution. They seemed to play the fool, and at dances sat on the ground near the Fon, pretending madness. They in fact acted as spies and were intelligent fellows.

They reached their destination; unfortunately a foolish Vai-boy let off his carbine, which could be heard at Bande. At dawn the Bali warriors came up. The army was divided into three. The centre was entrusted to a clever old sub-chief, and Tita N'yi and Tita M'bo each led a wing, to each of which 25 Vai were attached. The bulk of the Vai and the Europeans were in the centre. All agreed to meet in the market place at Bande.

Tita M'bo went off first with 1,500 men, to take Bande in the rear and prevent the Bande and Bafut from joining forces. Bande was on a low hill, about 1½km. long and ½ km. broad, with the market place in the middle, surrounded on three sides by a broad valley. The approach was made easier by a mist around the town.

About 2½ km. from the place, they came upon some women farming, who fled; so it seemed their approach was not expected, in spite of news received at Bangwa that nume-rous Bafut had come to join Bande. About 1,000 metres away from the town a halt was made to let the rear-guard come up. Meanwhile the Bande had seen them and their war-drums were heard, and their white banner waving denoted their willingness to fight. The German flag given them by von Spangenberg as a sign of friendship was nowhere to be seen.

After waiting for Tita N'yi to get into position, Zintgraff fired at the Bande flag-bearer and brought him down. This started the attack, and soon all order was lost in a general melee.

All pressed towards the market place where clouds of smoke from burning roofs made it hard to distinguish friend from foe. Here, before the palace, the Bande attempted a last, disciplined stand. The Bali flag-bearer had hardly stuck the tricolour in the stone-heap when the Bande from surrounding banana groves put up a heavy fire. They were, however, soon quietened by a counter-fusillade, and retired westwards. Some further fighting took place in the surrounding hills. Bande town was now inflames. Zintgraff saw numerous Bande regrouping north of the town, and on the hills to the north-east. In order to prevent being cut off from Ball on the way home, Zintgraff ordered his men to return to Bangwa with about 1,000 Ball by the shortest route. A group of Bande now took a group intending to return via Bafutchu in the flank, and Zintgraff climbed a hill to fire down on them. Trying to rejoin them he lost much time finding his way across a gulley. He now found himself in the rear of the right wing, so exhausted by his exertions that he could not move fast, or reach the main body to get it into disciplined order again. The Bande were meanwhile picking off stragglers. Had Zintgraff not been carried along by three Ball by turns, he would have been killed. Finally he reached the Bali at Bafutchu where two thirds of the Ball were assembled under the two princes. The rest of the Bali and the main Vai group had marched to Bangwa.

DISASTER

Zintgraff's attempts to rally the Bali to attack the Bande following them was contrary to local military usage, and failed. All were anxious to get back before nightfall to their town, which was unprotected. Zintgraff assumed that his own people must have reached Bangwa long ago and gone straight home. In the evening he himself reached Bali, went straight to Garega to report the news of the burning of Bande, and the 600 Bande casualties, and sent over to the station to report his return. Then came the unexpected news that nobody from the German expedition had returned. Bad news then began to trickle in of many Bali and Vai casualties near Bangwa, and finally that all four Europeans had been killed. Around midnight the greater part of his Vais returned, in very bad shape, and Zintgraff informed Garega, who came to the station with a dozen Bali who had brought the same tidings. It appeared that around 5 o'clock the Vais and the main part of the Bali left wing had been attacked by a larger force of Bande and Bafut who drove them back to Bangwa. The four Europeans had been surrounded and killed. The vassal towns of Bangwa, Bambutu and Bafutchu had changed sides and attacked the Bali and Vai resting and drinking in their houses. About 180 Bali and Vai had been killed thus. Hard as thdr losses were they were small in comparison with the loss of 1,500 vassals; this reduced the forces against Bande (5,000 warriors) and Bafut (8,000) to about 3-4,000. Zintgraff immediately handed over all the powder and flints of the trade expedition to Garega.

Zintgraff had little ammunition left. After the deaths of the Europeans the Vai carrier party had lost their heads and their ammunition packs had been lost to the enemy. He sent Caulwell and Carstensen, still sick, with the weaker Vai down to Babessong to get news of the expected munitions, and to get them up rapidly.

Vai was understandable as they had run out of ammunition. Lt. von Spangenberg, thinking the battle was over, had prevented the distribution of new ammunition. It was also clear that the Europeans, especially von Spangenberg, had been too exhausted to march away quickly.

Tita M'bo went out with a number of people to get news of Zintgraff's friends. He brought back the same story. He laid waste the treacherous towns and brought home some expedition stores from Bangwa, including Zintgraff's blanket.

Garega condoled with Zintgraff over his friends' deaths in a striking way. A little earth from the houses of the dead men was mixed with water in a bowl then Garega 'raising it in a solemn manner, full of natural decency and dignity, said "The white man's four friends are dead and I see sadness in his face. And since it is impossible for me to see his companions, I will drink some of the earth they have trodden in Bali so that even after their death they and I will have something in common".'

E. M. Chilver

Zintgraff's Officers

Freiherr von Steinaecker	L. Hendel	G. Conrau †††
N. Carstensen	Lt. von Spangenberg †	M. Huwe †
F. Caulwell ††	H. Nehber †	H. Tiedt †

† Killed at the Battle of Mankon, 31st January, 1891
†† Died, probably late 1891
††† Killed at Fontem, 1899

Garega was right in thinking Bande had no intention of attacking. For one thing the Bande chief had sent 30 of his wives to Bafut and Bafut was not letting them return to Bande.

The women of Bali now mourned the dead with cries—among them was the captain of Garegd's warriors.

From Babessong came the news that Caulwell and Carstensen were better but that there was no news of munitions from the coast, news which greatly embarrased Zintgraff.

An arms inspection at the Station revealed no more than 130 carbines and 2,000 bullets. The rest had been used or lost in the battle. Although Zintgr aff had sent a message to the coast on 8th February 1891, with his silver-topped walking stick as an emblem, he now felt it would be wiser to go to the coast himself, to find out what lay behind the Governor's silence. Garega guaranteed the safety of Carstensen, who was to stay behind with 200 men in Bali, while Caulwell was to come down to Banyang to establish a trading station there, which would also be an intelligence post, Zintgraff's Vai-boy shad recovered their morale, but most wanted to return with him. He left the most reliable behind with Carstensen and set out on the 12th February with Caulwell, 100 Vai and 40 Bali. Fo Bessong also gave 10 men to Zintgraff. Zintgraff stopped at Miyimbi's to arrange for the trade station, and Miyimbi gave him another 9 men to take to the coast.

The Banyang villages were deserted. At Fo Tabe's drinking house he found his walking stick and letter. A Banyang slave explained that Difang's people thought it was bad magic and held Zintgraff responsible for recent destruction of farms by elephants. Even the Bali believed that Zintgrajf had magical powers. It seemed evident also that the Bande battle, which Zintgraff thought was a failure, was locally regarded as a victory.

E. M. Chilver

RE-ORGANIZATION

The expedition arrived at Duala on 1st March 1891, to the surprise of the Governor who had believed rumours of its destruction, and had done nothing about Zintgraff's January despatch. The Governor took the line that Zintgraff's expedition was independent of the Kamerun administration and must look after itself. However, he was persuaded to allow the despatch to Bali of 120 men with rifles and considerable ammunition under the outstanding Jantzen and Thormahlen agent Conrau, who would replace Nehber.

Meanwhile Zintgraff sent a despatch to the Foreign Office asking for 2,000 Mausers to equip the Bah.

Though dane-guns would have satisfied the Bali, to give them away would have damaged trade. Moreover., the Ball, given Mausers, would have been dependent on the Germans for ammunition. Zintgraff also asked for replacements of the Europeans, as he and Carstensen could not manage alone. The Hamburg firm, however, was heart and soul in the enterprise and not only provided Conrau, but his successor the experienced African traveller Lucas Hendel. Zintgraff also asked permission to build a road from Mundame to Bah with the help of local tribes.

Zintgraff remarked however, that his plans were not received with much enthusiasm. The monopoly granted to Jantzen and Thormahlen had been broken, with Government permission, by the Duala traders, who were acting for English firms which reaped the benefits of German efforts. There were only two German firms in Duala and it was not surprising that the English ones were uninterested in replacing the Calabar outlet by Duala. The greater part of the trade goods in the interior were of English origin. Zintgraff's plans needed money. He returned to Barombi to prepare for road-making and await his helpers.

Carstensen sent regular and reassuring reports from Ball. On the 25th June 1891, the help arrived in the persons of Rittmeister von Gemmingen and Lt. F. Hutter, with 2,000 rifles.

A TREATY WTTH GAREGA

The transport of the munitions to Baliburg was attended with great difficulties, as the rainy season was earlier than usual, and there were too few carriers. But things improved after Garega sent down 3,000 men to Caulwe's station at Miyimbi. On 23rd August Zintgraff returned to Bali with Hutter, leaving von Gemmingen to follow. Their appearance was followed by the arrival of embassies from two large tribes neighbouring Bande with gifts and requests for friendly relations. In the first week after their arrival Zintgraff discussed the terms of a treaty with Garega and did his best to explain its terms in detail.

These were as follows:

'In order to bring the Bali tribe to such power and influence as will enable it to lead the tribes in northern Kamerun, the following persons, namely Garega as an independent Chief speaking for himself and his people and Dr Zintgraff as Commissioner of the German Government, make the following treaty subject to the approval of the latter:

1.—Garega will transfer to Dr Zintgraff such powers as he at present exercises in the lands, namely the right over life and limb and the final decisions as to war and peace.
2.—Accordingly Garega undertakes to give effect to such orders as may be given by Dr Zintgraff in the interest of the Bali and secure their acceptance, likewise to

carry out penalties inflicted by Dr Zintgraff himself or to comply loyally with their execution by other means, and finally to hold his forces in unconditional readiness for any war Dr Zintgraff may consider necessary and not to undertake war for his own advantage and without Dr Zintgraff's concurrence.

3.—In consideration of this the establishment, recognition and protection of Garega's position as the paramount Chief of the surrounding tribes of the northern Kamerun hinterland will be secured.

4.—The proceeds of regular tax to be raised from the neighbouring tribes and a fixed duty payable by caravans passing through the Bali districts from the hinterland will be divided between Dr Zintgraff and Garega to defray the costs of administration in North-Kamerun, the part due to Dr Zintgraff to be used for direct Government costs such as road and bridge building, supplementation of weapons and ammunition, provisioning of the Station etc. and the part due to Garega to be regarded as an official payment for loyal compliance with the terms of the treaty now concluded.

5.—The regulation of the incidence of these taxes, the establishment of customs stations and appointment of customs officers and connected regulations are to be decided in accordance with the wishes of Dr Zintgraff.

This treaty was later recognised by the Foreign Office.' Lt. Hutter reported as follows to the Foreign Office on the celebrations following the conclusion of the treaty:

To start with the conversations took place under circumstances similar to those at home, but through double interpretation. Dr Zintgraff said something in English to our interpreter who repeated it in Vai to Fonte who repeated it in Bali to the King— and the answer was made likewise. The King in discussing it with his retainers and councillors used a private language. Soon it came to the point. The contents of the paper were read to the King and explained thus: Dr Zintgraff, or when he is not here or no longer here, Lt. Hutter, and the next white man after him etc. has powers of life and death in Bali and power to inflict punishment, decides on peace and war and the tribute to be exacted from conquered tribes, and deals with all inter-tribal disputes— these were the main points of the very comprehensive treaty. The King put his mark on it with unpracticed hand—3 crosses which he obstinately insisted on putting on both sides of the large sheet. As witness I put my signature below. Then he stood and fired his gun, which his followers did also.

Dr Zintgraff and I went out into the market-place, with us the King's speakers Fonte and Tituat. The King remained behind, for it was the white man who now stood before the people. A hen was brought and the speaker called for silence. The large crowd heard the King's message in perfect silence. A man then brought some pepper which Zintgraff chewed and spat into the beak of the hen. Then the speaker went, holding the hen by the legs, and brushed its head along the long rows of guns, shouting the while. Then he came back to us and Dr Zintgraff had to take the hen, whirl it round his head and dash it to pieces against the stone-pyramid. Then five shots rang out and the ceremony was over. Its meaning was that the fighting power of Bali belonged to the whites.'

Zintgraff and Hutter inspected the warriors, and Hutter notes they had 700 breech-loaders and 1,000 done-guns. Hutter thought that if they could be taught musketry hs could trust them[l] to fetch the Devil out of Hell.' Both then returned to drink with the Fon. Hutter was reminded of the mead-feasts of the Norse heroes.

E. M. Chilver

THE BALI-TRUPPE

Bafut and Bande were now reported to be willing to make peace. Although they could now have been destroyed this was not Zintgraff's desire and did not accord with the policy of making Bali the leading power. The Bande however refused to hand over the bodies of the four Europeans as a mark of peaceful intentions.

Hutter started training 200 Bali as soldiers, since von Gemmingen had been sent to Edea, where he soon died. European staff was short for all the tasks required, road-building, training, and work at the station. Zintgraff's request for more staff went unheeded until, on 26th December, 1891, Lt. von Steinacker came as assistant to Hutter and also the road-builder, Bockner; with them came the order that any further advance to Chad must stop.

The Bali soldiers, unused to discipline, complained to Zintgraff that the native sergeant yelled at them, but when the words of command and their purpose was explained, they were pacified. They made good progress. In April, 1892, a demonstration was made before Bagangu. Here flutter's little troop were to await reinforcements. Since it was impos-sible to mobilise the Bali irregulars, the influential Tita N'yi came with the message they were to return, and called on the soldiers to follow him. Hutter had no written confirmation and refused to budge, and so did his troop— a good example of discipline. It proved hard to convince Ball noblemen that their dependents could not be bought off, or that the soldiers could not be ordered by them to fetch palmwine, etc.

Hutter was impressed by the military qualities of the Bali, who responded well to an understanding commander. So keen were they that they continued training and drilling each other during the rainy season.

PROGRESS

Zintgraff continued his negotiations with Bafut and Bande, and it seemed clear that Bafut was in earnest. Fon Gualem's confidential servant told Garega that he was ready for blood-brotherhood, and he sent a gift of ivory. Bande remained obstinate, and Zintgraff thought that the best policy was to isolate it. Meanwhile the neighbouring Bamunda and Bafuen entered into protection agreements sanctified by blood-friendship, while Bagam and Banssoa sent along embassies.

These favourable developments were hindered by the outbreak of a serious epidemic, perhaps dysentery, in Bali. Garega and his councillors were convinced that this was due to witchcraft, and put people through the sasswood poison-ordeal, which killed many. Zintgraff upbraided Garega for his folly; here was Bali weakened by sickness and now he was weakening it further by ritual killing—Bande would be delighted. Garega saw the point at once, threw away the sasswood, and supported Zintgraff's sanitary and medical measures; a thorough clean-up of the town took place, indoor burials were prohibited, and the sick were dosed with a simple 'bitters'. The sickness passed and Zintgraff's influence with Garega increased.

Relations with the Kamerun administration remained uneasy. Zintgraff thought he must settle this before the rainy season of 1892 and also bring up some presents for the new allies. As it was he had hardly enough money to pay his soldiers.

In April, the non-commissioned officers Knetschke, Wisotzki, Goger and Ehmann and the agriculturists Neumann and Nette arrived to take charge of the road-building programme and the security of the route. It was obvious that connections between coast and hinterland could not be undertaken by an independent expedition without backing, and that interests would clash unless co-operation was arranged. Zintgraff went with von Steinacker into the forest in May to establish intermediate points along the route.

In May/June 1892 Tinto was established, with the help of Bali and Babessong, not far from the Jantzen and Thormahlen factory. Thence he went to Mundame to develop it as a supply-centre for the expedition. Here also was a Jantzen and Thormahlen factory, and here too, Bali helped to build the station and were now freely using the route. Thus were the objects of the expedition fulfilled. Unarmed messengers could now cover the 200 km. Bali-Mundame road in 5 days. The hold of the middleman was broken, and the inland tribes, Bali included, had seen, in Mundame, how they could sell their produce for higher prices. Numerous Grassfielders had been to the coast and seen the Governor and the factories.

ZIMMERER'S OPPOSITION

But the coast people, sensing the Governor's coldness to Zintgraff, made capital out of it, and Zintgraff's own people remarked & Massa, them Governor no like you.' The Bali were 'a thorn in the eye' to the Duala, who had lost their chance of profiteering at the expense of the inland tribes. When Zintgraff sent some Bali to Duala under von Steinacker they were set upon simultaneously in several villages and three were killed. In spite of Zintgraff's representations the Governor did not pursue the guilty, or make any proper inquiry. Zintgraff felt that a wrong had been done, and that the whole aim of opening up a safe route between the coast and the hinterland was in jeopardy.

He was determined to secure the intervention of the home Government, and managed to pacify the angry Bait by telling them he was going to lay the matter before the Kaiser. He asked them to await his return quietly, though Garega wanted to send an embassy to the Kaiser. Zintgraff took the first steamer to Germany to present his case to the Foreign Office.

The Foreign Office turned out to be solidly on the Governor's side. Zintgraff resigned and within a year Hutter and von Steinacker also had left Kamerun. Unwilling, however, to waste his work, he prepared a plan with a private concern, which involved the recruitment of Bali for the plantations, the establishment of peasant villages on the Bali-Mundame road, and scientific research: Zintgraff asked in a letter to the Foreign Office that this concern should be free of import duties.

On 10th August, 1893, the Foreign Office replied firmly and curtly that Zintgraff could be given no special facilities, and moreover he was forbidden to return to Kamerun because his presence would be disturbing and affect the prestige of the Governor. This might be reconsidered in two years.

Meanwhile, while Zintgraff was contriving his return, all the stations from Ball town to Mundame, and the road-building programme, were given up. At Mundame, however, the Jantzen and Thormahlen factory remained.

Selected Bibliography

German

Max Esser *An der Westkuste Afrikas*, Berlin, 1898. Describes journey to Bali in 1896.

Franz Hutter *Wanderungen und Forschungen im Nord-Hinterland von Kamerun*, Braunschweig, 1902.

Wilhelm Kemner *Kamerun*, Berlin, 1938. Deals with the origins of W.A.P.V. and Zintgraff's part in it.

Jesko von Puttkamer *Gouverneursjahre in Kamerun*, Berlin, 1912.

Eugen Zintgraff *Nord-Kamerun*, Berlin, 1895.

English

Edwin Ardener *Coastal Bantu of the Cameroons*, Eth. Survey of Africa, Western Africa, Pt. ix, International African Institute, London, 1956. Contains a survey of the Kpe-Mboko, Duala-Limba and Tanga-Yasa groups.

Historical Notes on the Scheduled Monuments of West Cameroon, Buea, 1965. Summarizes German material.

E. W. and S. Ardener and W. A. Warmington *Plantation and Village in the Cameroons*, Oxford, 1960. Gives a brief account of the growth of the plantations in the last chapters.

E. M. Chilver and P. M. Kaberry 'From Tribute to Tax in a Tikar chiefdom', *Africa*, xxx, No. 1, 1960.

Phyllis M. Kaberry Traditional Politics in Nsaw', *Africa*, xxix, No. 4, 1959.

P. M. *Kaberry* and E. M. Chilver 'An Outline of the Traditional Political System of Bali-Nyonga, Southern Cameroons', *Africa*, October, 1961.

A.H.M. Kirk-Greene Adamawa Past and Present, Oxford, 1957. Contains some brief notes on German exploration and policy.

M. McCulloch, M. Littlewood and I. Dugast *Peoples of the Central Cameroons*, Eth. Survey of Africa, Western Africa, Pt. ix, International African Institute, London, 1954. Contains a brief survey of the Tikar, Bamum, Bamileke and Banen peoples.

Harry R. Rudin *Germans in the Cameroons, 1884-1914*, London, 1938. The best modern account of the period. For those embarking on the collection of oral traditions, we recommend.

J. Vansina 'Recording the Oral Tradition of the Bakuba, I. Methods', *African History*, C.U.P. I, No. I, pp. 43-51, 1960.

Titles by *Langaa* RPCIG

Francis B. Nyamnjoh
Stories from Abakwa
Mind Searching
The Disillusioned African
The Convert
Souls Forgotten
Married But Available
Intimate Strangers

Dibussi Tande
No Turning Back. Poems of Freedom 1990-1993
Scribbles from the Den: Essays on Politics and Collective Memory in Cameroon

Kangsen Feka Wakai
Fragmented Melodies

Ntemfac Ofege
Namondo. Child of the Water Spirits
Hot Water for the Famous Seven

Emmanuel Fru Doh
Not Yet Damascus
The Fire Within
Africa's Political Wastelands: The Bastardization of Cameroon
Oriki'badan
Wading the Tide
Stereotyping Africa: Surprising Answers to Surprising Questions

Thomas Jing
Tale of an African Woman

Peter Wuteh Vakunta
Grassfields Stories from Cameroon
Green Rape: Poetry for the Environment
Majunga Tok: Poems in Pidgin English
Cry, My Beloved Africa
No Love Lost
Straddling The Mungo: A Book of Poems in English & French

Ba'bila Mutia
Coils of Mortal Flesh

Kehbuma Langmia
Titabet and the Takumbeng
An Evil Meal of Evil
The Earth Mother

Victor Elame Musinga
The Barn
The Tragedy of Mr. No Balance

Ngessimo Mathe Mutaka
Building Capacity: Using TEFL and African Languages as Development-oriented Literacy Tools

Milton Krieger
Cameroon's Social Democratic Front: Its History and Prospects as an Opposition Political Party, 1990-2011

Sammy Oke Akombi
The Raped Amulet
The Woman Who Ate Python
Beware the Drives: Book of Verse
The Wages of Corruption

Susan Nkwentie Nde
Precipice
Second Engagement

Francis B. Nyamnjoh & Richard Fonteh Akum
The Cameroon GCE Crisis: A Test of Anglophone Solidarity

Joyce Ashuntantang & Dibussi Tande
Their Champagne Party Will End! Poems in Honor of Bate Besong

Emmanuel Achu
Disturbing the Peace

Rosemary Ekosso
The House of Falling Women

Peterkins Manyong
God the Politician

George Ngwane
The Power in the Writer: Collected Essays on Culture, Democracy & Development in Africa

John Percival
The 1961 Cameroon Plebiscite: Choice or Betrayal

Albert Azeyeh
Réussite scolaire, faillite sociale : généalogie mentale de la crise de l'Afrique noire francophone

Aloysius Ajab Amin & Jean-Luc Dubois
Croissance et développement au Cameroun : d'une croissance équilibrée à un développement équitable

Carlson Anyangwe
Imperialistic Politics in Cameroun:
Resistance & the Inception of the Restoration of the Statehood of Southern Cameroons
Betrayal of Too Trusting a People: The UN, the UK and the Trust Territory of the Southen Cameroons

Bill F. Ndi
K'Cracy, Trees in the Storm and Other Poems
Map: Musings On Ars Poetica
Thomas Lurting: The Fighting Sailor Turn'd Peaceable / Le marin combattant devenu paisible
Soleil et ombre

Kathryn Toure, Therese Mungah Shalo Tchombe & Thierry Karsenti
ICT and Changing Mindsets in Education

Charles Alobwed'Epie
The Day God Blinked
The Bad Samaritan
The Lady with the Sting
What a Next of Kin!

G. D. Nyamndi
Babi Yar Symphony
Whether losing, Whether winning
Tussles: Collected Plays
Dogs in the Sun

Samuel Ebelle Kingue
Si Dieu était tout un chacun de nous ?

Ignasio Malizani Jimu
Urban Appropriation and Transformation: bicycle, taxi and handcart operators in Mzuzu, Malawi

Justice Nyo' Wakai
Under the Broken Scale of Justice: The Law and My Times

John Eyong Mengot
A Pact of Ages

Ignasio Malizani Jimu
Urban Appropriation and Transformation: Bicycle Taxi and Handcart Operators

Joyce B. Ashuntantang
Landscaping and Coloniality: The Dissemination of Cameroon Anglophone Literature
A Basket of Flaming Ashes

Jude Fokwang
Mediating Legitimacy: Chieftaincy and Democratisation in Two African Chiefdoms

Michael A. Yanou
Dispossession and Access to Land in South Africa: an African Perspevctive

Tikum Mbah Azonga
Cup Man and Other Stories
The Wooden Bicycle and Other Stories

John Nkemngong Nkengasong
Letters to Marions (And the Coming Generations)
The Call of Blood

Amady Aly Dieng
Les étudiants africains et la littérature négro-africaine d'expression française

Tah Asongwed
Born to Rule: Autobiography of a life President
Child of Earth

Frida Menkan Mbunda
Shadows From The Abyss

Bongasu Tanla Kishani
A Basket of Kola Nuts
Konglanjo (Spears of Love without Ill-fortune) and Letters to Ethiopia with some Random Poems

Fo Angwafo III S.A.N of Mankon
Royalty and Politics: The Story of My Life

Basil Diki
The Lord of Anomy
Shrouded Blessings

Churchill Ewumbue-Monono
Youth and Nation-Building in Cameroon: A Study of National Youth Day Messages and Leadership Discourse (1949-2009)

Emmanuel N. Chia, Joseph C. Suh & Alexandre Ndeffo Tene
Perspectives on Translation and Interpretation in Cameroon

Linus T. Asong
The Crown of Thorns
No Way to Die
A Legend of the Dead: Sequel of *The Crown of Thorns*
The Akroma File
Salvation Colony: Sequel to *No Way to Die*
Chopchair
Doctor Frederick Ngenito
The Crabs of Bangui

Vivian Sihshu Yenika
Imitation Whiteman
Press Lake Varsity Girls: The Freshman Year

Beatrice Fri Bime
Someplace, Somewhere
Mystique: A Collection of Lake Myths

Shadrach A. Ambanasom
Son of the Native Soil
The Cameroonian Novel of English Expression: An Introduction
Education of the Deprived: Anglophone Cameroon Literary Drama
Homage and Courtship *(Romantic Stirrings of a Yourng Man)*

Tangie Nsoh Fonchingong and Gemandze John Bobuin
Cameroon: The Stakes and Challenges of Governance and Development

Tatah Mentan
Democratizing or Reconfiguring Predatory Autocracy? Myths and Realities in Africa Today

Roselyne M. Jua & Bate Besong
To the Budding Creative Writer: A Handbook

Albert Mukong
Prisonner without a Crime: Disciplining Dissent in Ahidjo's Cameroon

Mbuh Tennu Mbuh
In the Shadow of my Country

Bernard Nsokika Fonlon
Genuine Intellectuals: Academic and Social Responsibilities of Universities in Africa

Lilian Lem Atanga
Gender, Discourse and Power in the Cameroonian Parliament

Cornelius Mbifung Lambi & Emmanuel Neba Ndenecho
Ecology and Natural Resource Development in the Western Highlands of Cameroon: Issues in Natural Resource Managment

Gideon F. For-mukwai
Facing Adversity with Audacity

Peter W. Vakunta & Bill F. Ndi
Nul n'a le monopole du français : deux poètes du Cameroon anglophone

Emmanuel Matateyou
Les murmures de l'harmattan

Ekpe Inyang
The Hill Barbers

JK Bannavti
Rock of God *(Kílàn ke Nyǜy)*

Godfrey B. Tangwa (Rotcod Gobata)
I Spit on their Graves: Testimony Relevant to the Democratization Struggle in Cameroon
Road Companion to Democracy and Meritocracy *(Further Essays from an African Perspective)*

Henrietta Mambo Nyamnjoh
"We Get Nothing from Fishishing", Fishing for Boat Opportunies amongst Senegalese Fisher Migrants

Bill F. Ndi, Dieurat Clervoyant & Peter W. Vakunta
Les douleurs de la plume noire : du Cameroun anglophone à Haïti

Laurence Juma
Kileleshwa: A Tale of Love, Betrayal and Corruption in Kenya

Nol Alembong
Forest Echoes (Poems)

Marie-Hélène Mottin-Sylla & Joëlle Palmieri
Excision : les jeunes changent l'Afrique par les TIC

Walter Gam Nkwi
Voicing the Voiceless: Contributions to Closing Gaps in Cameroon History, 1958-2009

John Koyela Fokwang
A Dictionary of Popular Bali Names

Alain-Joseph Sissao
(Translated from the French by Nina Tanti)
Folktales from the Moose of Burkina Faso

Colin Ayeab Diyen
The Earth in Peril

E. M. Chilver
Zintgraff's Explorations in Bamenda, Adamawa and the Benue Lands 1889—1892